Public Images, Private Readings: Multi-Perspective Approaches to the Post-Palaeolithic Rock Art

Proceedings of the XVII UISPP World Congress (1–7 September 2014, Burgos, Spain)

Volume 5 / Session A11e

Edited by

Ramón Fábregas Valcarce and Carlos Rodríguez-Rellán

Archaeopress Archaeology

Archaeopress Publishing Ltd
Gordon House
276 Banbury Road
Oxford OX2 7ED

www.archaeopress.com

ISBN 978 1 78491 289 5
ISBN 978 1 78491 290 1 (e-Pdf)

© Archaeopress, UISPP and authors 2016

Cover image: Petroglyph of Fonte da Pena Furada VII, Campo Lameiro (Galicia, Spain)
3D model by Alia Vázquez Martínez, Miguel Carrero Pazos, Benito Vilas Estévez
(University of Santiago de Compostela)

VOLUME EDITORS: Ramón FÁBREGAS VALCARCE, Carlos RODRÍGUEZ-RELLÁN

SERIES EDITOR: The board of UISPP

SERIES PROPERTY: UISPP – International Union of Prehistoric and Protohistoric Sciences

The editing of this volume was funded by the Instituto Terra e Memória, Centro de Geociências UID/Multi/00073/2013, with the support of the Fundação para a Ciência e Tecnologia FCT/MEC

KEY-WORDS IN THIS VOLUME: Audience – Landscape – Digital imaging – GIS analysis – Rock Art

UISPP PROCEEDINGS SERIES is a printed on demand and an open access publication, edited by UISPP through Archaeopress

BOARD OF UISPP: Jean Bourgeois (President), Luiz Oosterbeek (Secretary-General),
François Djindjian (Treasurer), Ya-Mei Hou (Vice President), Marta Arzarello (Deputy Secretary-General).
The Executive Committee of UISPP also includes the Presidents of all the international scientific commissions (www.uispp.org)

BOARD OF THE XVII WORLD CONGRESS OF UISPP: Eudald Carbonell (Secretary-General),
Robert Sala I Ramos, Jose Maria Rodriguez Ponga (Deputy Secretary-Generals)

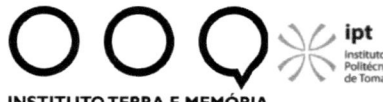 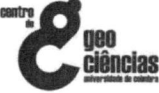 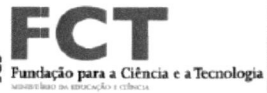 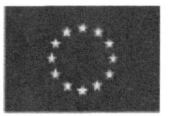

All rights reserved. No part of this book may be reproduced, or transmitted, in any form or by any means, electronic, mechanical, photocopying or otherwise, without the prior written permission of the copyright owners.

This book is available direct from Archaeopress or from our website www.archaeopress.com

Contents

List of Figures and Tables ii

Foreword to the XVII UISPP Congress Proceedings Series Edition iv
Luiz OOSTERBEEK

Introduction v
Ramón FÁBREGAS VALCARCE and Carlos RODRÍGUEZ-RELLÁN

Stones before stones. Reused stelae and menhirs in Galician megaliths 1
P. BUENO RAMIREZ, F. CARRERA RAMIREZ, R. DE BALBÍN BEHRMANN,
R. BARROSO BERMEJO, X. DARRIBA and A. PAZ

**Illustrating the Sabor Valley (Trás-os-Montes, Portugal):
rock art and its long-term diachrony since the Upper Palaeolithic
until the Iron Age** 17
Sofia SOARES DE FIGUEIREDO, Pedro XAVIER, Dário NEVES, José MACIEL,
Luís NOBRE and Isabel DOMÍNGUEZ GARCÍA

**Archaeological field survey in the *Erqueyez* site (Western Sahara):
new discoveries of rock art** 29
Teresa MUÑIZ LÓPEZ, Ahmed KHATRI, David GARCÍA GONZÁLEZ and Carmina LÓPEZ-RODRÍGUEZ

**Measuring the spatially-related perceptibility of prehistoric rock art.
Some initial notes** 41
Carlos RODRÍGUEZ-RELLÁN and Ramón FÁBREGAS VALCARCE

**The paintings of "oculadas" figures in the Neolithic and Chalcolithic of Northern Portugal:
the study case of Serra de Passos** 51
Maria DE JESUS SANCHES

***Going by the numbers*, a quantitative approach to the Galician prehistoric petroglyphs** 63
Alia VÁZQUEZ MARTÍNEZ, Ramón FÁBREGAS VALCARCE and Carlos RODRÍGUEZ-RELLÁN

List of Figures and Tables

P. Bueno Ramirez et al.: **Stones before stones. Reused stelae and menhirs in Galician megaliths**

Figure 1. Precise location of the sites mentioned in this paper 2
Figure 2. Some examples of triangular stelae found in the Galician megaliths' context 4
Figure 3. "The Thing" sequence. Red paint and engravings in *Casa dos Mouros* (Galicia) and
  Mané Rutual (Britany) 5
Figure 4. Plans from *Forno dos Mouros, Os Muiños* and *Dombate* 6
Figure 5. The anthropomorphic stelae from *Dombate* 7
Figure 6. An example of some plans of Galician megaliths 7
Figure 7. Reused stelae and menhirs within the Iberian Peninsula 8
Figure 8. Reused uprights with technic sequences: stelae from *Castiñeiras* and
  stelae of *Monte dos Marxos* 11
Figure 9. *Bico de Lagos* cist 12
Table 1. Activity Beneath the burial mounds construction, and evidences
  of the burial mounds mass in Galicia's megaliths 3
Table 2. Evidences of the extension phases on the mounds and stelae and
  menhirs reemployed in Galicia's megaliths 9

S. Soares de Figueiredo et al.: **Illustrating the Sabor Valley (Trás-os-Montes, Portugal): rock art and its long-term diachrony since the Upper Palaeolithic until the Iron Age**

Figure 1. Localization of the archaeological sites in the Sabor Valley 19
Figure 2. Engraved plaques from the Foz do Medal terrace 21
Figure 3. Rock art sites of Ribeira da Pedra de Asma 7, Santo Antão da Barca
  and Veado do Cabeço do Aguilhão 23
Figure 4. Engraved plaques from Crestelos 24
Figure 5. Graphs indicating the percentage of figurative motifs 26

T. Muñiz López et al.: **Archaeological field survey in the *Erqueyez* site (Western Sahara): new discoveries of rock art**

Figure 1. View of the west side of the massif of Erqueyez Lemgasem 30
Figure 2. Map showing the location of the shelters 32
Figure 3. Detail of graphic manifestations of human figures in Shelter 1 33
Figure 4. Calque of the representations that are documented in Shelter 1 33
Figure 5. Detail of graphic manifestations of human figures in Shelter 2 34
Figure 6. Calque of the representations that are documented in the Shelter 2 34
Figure 7. Calque of the representations that are documented in the Shelter 3 35
Figure 8. Details of graphic manifestations of animals figures in Shelter 4 35
Figure 9. Calque of the representations that are documented in the Shelter 4 35
Figure 10. Calque of the representations that are documented in the Shelter 5 36
Figure 11. Calque of the representations that are documented in the Shelter 6 36
Figure 12. Detail of graphic demonstrations in the Shelter 7 37
Figure 13. Calque of the representations that are documented in the Shelter 7 37
Figure 14. Calque of the representations that are documented in the Shelter 8 38
Figure 15. View from inside the Shelter 8 38

C. Rodríguez-Rellán and R. Fábregas Valcarce: **Measuring the spatially-related perceptibility of prehistoric rock art. Some initial notes**

Figure 1. Least-cost path network linking different points of the Barbanza Peninsula 44
Figure 2. 'Inverse viewshed' or cumulative viewshed carried out from the least cost paths 46
Figure 3. Percentage of petroglyphs perceived from the major pathways
  calculated using GRASS GIS 47

FIGURE 4. MINIMUM DISTANCE OF PETROGLYPHS THAT WERE AND WERE NOT PERCEIVED
FROM THE MAJOR PATHWAYS 48

M. DE JESUS SANCHES: **The paintings of "oculadas" figures in the Neolithic and Chalcolithic of Northern Portugal: the study case of Serra de Passos**

FIGURE 1. GEOGRAPHICAL LOCATION OF THE PASSOS MOUNTAIN IN THE NORTH OF PORTUGAL 52
FIGURE 2. COMPOSITION OF "OCULADOS" IDOL-LIKE FIGURES 53
FIGURE 3. "OCULADOS" IDOL-LIKE FIGURES 56
FIGURE 4. CERAMIC VASE WITH "OCULADA" DECORATION 58

A. VÁZQUEZ MARTÍNEZ et al.: *Going by the numbers*, **a quantitative approach to the Galician prehistoric petroglyphs**

FIGURE 1. STATE OF THE KNOWLEDGE ABOUT THE DISTRIBUTION OF ROCK ART IN GALICIA 64
FIGURE 2. DISTRIBUTION OF THE GALICIAN PETROGLYPHS 66
TABLE 1. NUMBER AND PERCENTAGE OF SITES WHERE THE DIFFERENT MOTIFS ARE PRESENT 67

Foreword to the XVII UISPP Congress Proceedings Series Edition

Luiz OOSTERBEEK
Secretary-General

UISPP has a long history, starting with the old International Association of Anthropology and Archaeology, back in 1865, until the foundation of UISPP itself in Bern, in 1931, and its growing relevance after WWII, from the 1950's. We also became members of the International Council of Philosophy and Human Sciences, associate of UNESCO, in 1955.

In its XIVth world congress in 2001, in Liège, UISPP started a reorganization process that was deepened in the congresses of Lisbon (2006) and Florianópolis (2011), leading to its current structure, solidly anchored in more than twenty-five international scientific commissions, each coordinating a major cluster of research within six major chapters: Historiography, methods and theories; Culture, economy and environments; Archaeology of specific environments; Art and culture; Technology and economy; Archaeology and societies.

The XVIIth world congress of 2014, in Burgos, with the strong support of Fundación Atapuerca and other institutions, involved over 1700 papers from almost 60 countries of all continents. The proceedings, edited in this series but also as special issues of specialized scientific journals, will remain as the most important outcome of the congress.

Research faces growing threats all over the planet, due to lack of funding, repressive behavior and other constraints. UISPP moves ahead in this context with a strictly scientific programme, focused on the origins and evolution of humans, without conceding any room to short term agendas that are not root in the interest of knowledge.

In the long run, which is the terrain of knowledge and science, not much will remain from the contextual political constraints, as severe or dramatic as they may be, but the new advances into understanding the human past and its cultural diversity will last, this being a relevant contribution for contemporary and future societies.

This is what UISPP is for, and this is also why we are currently engaged in contributing for the relaunching of Human Sciences in their relations with social and natural sciences, namely collaborating with the International Year of Global Understanding, in 2016, and with the World Conference of the Humanities, in 2017.

The next two congresses of UISPP, in Melbourne (2017) and in Geneva (2020), will confirm this route.

Introduction

Ramón FÁBREGAS VALCARCE, Carlos RODRÍGUEZ-RELLÁN

A significant number of Holocene societies throughout the world have resorted at one time or another to the making of paints or carvings on different places (tombs, rock-shelters or caves, open-air outcrops). The aim of the session "A11e. Public images, private readings: multi-perspective approaches to the post-Palaeolithic rock art", which was held within the XVII World UISPP Congress (Burgos, September 1-7 2014), was to put together the experiences of specialists from different areas of the Iberian Peninsula and the World. The approaches ranged from the archaeological definition of the artistic phenomena and their socioeconomic background to those concerning themselves with the symbolic and ritual nature of those practices, including the definition of the audience to which the graphic manifestations were addressed and the potential role of the latter in the making up of social identities and the enforcement of territorial claims. More empirical issues, such as new recording methodologies and data management or even dating were also considered during this session.

The papers presented at the session might be grouped in three sections: those dealing with the objectification/quantification of the graphic record and here would fit that by A. Vázquez *et alii*, aiming at the elaboration of a first general inventory of the Galician prehistoric art (North-western Spain), charting the variability of its manifestations.

A second group of papers has to do with the actual insertion of the prehistoric art in the wider landscape: Rodríguez-Rellán & Fábregas deal with the question of the alleged association of Galician petroglyphs to the natural routes and certain resource-rich areas by mobilizing techniques such as GIS applications.

The last section has to do with several case studies, where biographic, continuity and symbolic aspects may be ascertained. In Bueno *et alii*, the authors deal with the possible existence of megalithic stelae prior to the raising of megalithic chambers that quite often reused some of the former. One of the most talked-upon themes in the Iberian art belonging to the Neolithic and Copper Age, that of masks and eye motifs and their presence in N Portugal is addressed in Sanches's paper. Also dealing with the prehistoric art of N Portugal is Figueiredo *et alii's* presentation, this time centering on the Sabor valley whose CRM archaeology has yielded a vast number of art manifestations, otherwise ranging from the Upper Palaeolithic to the Iron Age. Finally, Muñiz-López *et alii* report on their survey carried out in an all too-forgotten area, Western Sahara, that has produced a large number of new painted shelters, adding significantly to the catalogue of graphisms already known there.

Stones before stones. Reused stelae and menhirs in Galician megaliths

P. Bueno-Ramirez
Area de Prehistoria. Universidad de Alcalá de Henares

F. Carrera-Ramirez
Escola Superior de Conservación e Restauración de Bens Culturais de Galicia

R. de Balbín-Behrmann, R. Barroso-Bermejo
Area de Prehistoria. Universidad de Alcalá de Henares

X. Darriba
Centro de Investigación del Museo de Prehistoria y Arqueología de Cantabria (MUPAC)

A. Paz

Abstract

Reused stelae and menhirs confirm previous roles and reinforce the interest of analysing the monument's biography through each slab's history. These sequences offer two very interesting options for interpretation in Galicia. Firstly, the mentioned archaeological evidences, the pre-existing structures found beneath the tumulus, are an indication of events that happened before building the monuments. Old stelae and menhirs could be linked to this first stage and could have been the very reason for the beginning of the construction; this idea is supported in Galicia by the direct chronologies of the uprights. There is another yet unpublished argument that will add to the evaluation so these sequences. By studying the painted decoration, it is feasible to read chronologies and to define maintenance phases including engravings. The ideology expressed by these ritual expressions multiplies the applicable approaches for the study of a social framework that supports the process of megaliths building around Europe.

Key words: *Megalithic art. Galicia. Stele. Menhir*

Resumen

Estelas y menhires reutilizados confirman papeles anteriores, reforzando el interés del análisis de la biografía de los monumentos, a partir de los recorridos individualizados de cada una de las piezas que los componen. Estas secuencias tienen en Galicia dos argumentos muy valiosos: estructuras bajo túmulo que aportan indicios de eventos anteriores a la construcción con los que pueden estar relacionados las estelas y menhires que sirvieron de arranque para nuevas construcciones, y la documentación de fechas C14 sobre los pigmentos de sus decoraciones. La superposición de técnicas aporta un género de argumentos inéditos al estudio de la diacronía de los megalitos, no sólo por lo que se refiere a sus momentos más antiguos, sino a los diferentes eventos de manutención y refactura. De ahí que el estudio detallado de los programas gráficos megalíticos, proponga un punto de inflexión sobre las posibilidades de este género de aplicaciones metodológicas al resto de Europa.

Palabras clave: *Arte Megalítico. Galicia. Estelas. Menhires*

The study of European megaliths has come through multiple phases, from searching for objects to developing stratigraphic sequences and analysing their architectural complexities. Proving that megaliths are the result of continuous transformations is currently one of the most original approaches (Bueno *et al.* 2007a; Laporte, 2010). Recent works within the Iberian Peninsula have focused on identifying actual burial settings, recognisable scenes where ideological patterns can be understood.

The development of a specific methodology (Bueno *et al.* 2012, 2014; Carrera, 1997; Carrera *et al.* 2005; Carrera, 2011) added to the increasing technical possibilities available for sites in the Iberian Peninsula where prehistoric art is found, constitute a considerable data increment.

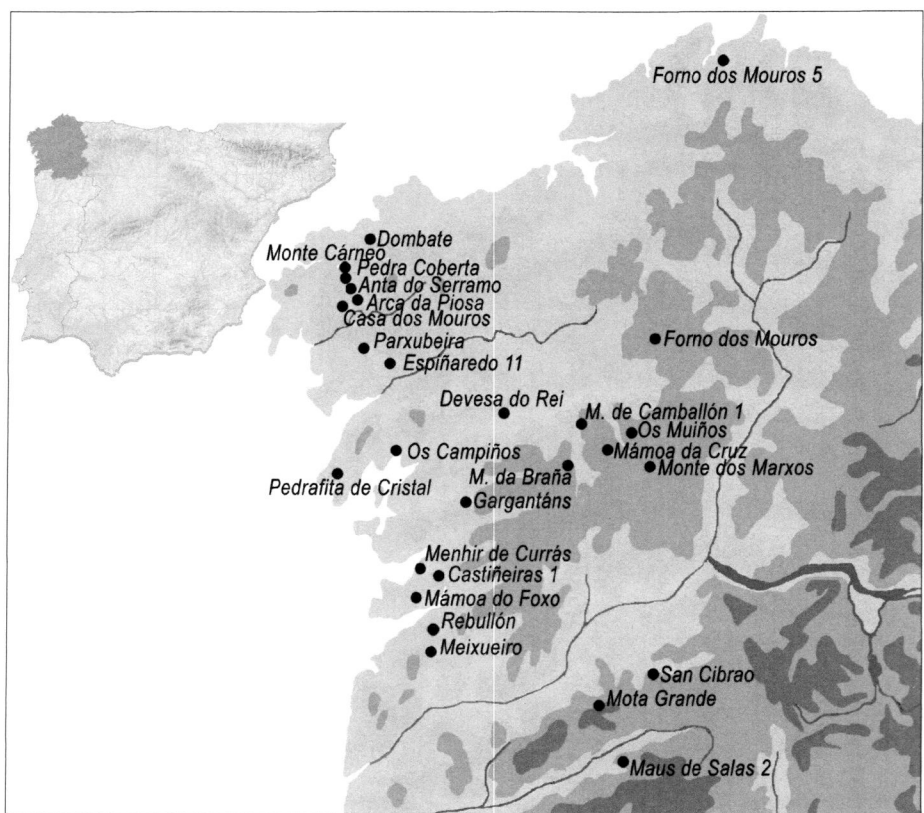

FIGURE 1. PRECISE LOCATION OF THE SITES MENTIONED IN THIS PAPER.

The most outstanding novelties and their correspondent specialized teams are found within two Iberian areas: Northwest and South-southwest. Furthermore the quality and interest of both the Cantabrian area and the Northeast provide more references for the Neolithic and Chalcolithic *ex-novo* and reused burial sites striking abundance (Bueno *et al.* 2009; Bueno *et al.* 2013), which place the Iberian Peninsula as one of the richest areas in Europe.

This paper will discuss the role of the new material found in Galicia in relation to the current historiographical argument. New C14 dates –obtained from organic matter sampled from the pigments that constitute the decoration of some uprights (Carrera, Fábregas 2002, 2008; Steelman *et al.* 2005) – and archaeological contexts present a unique approach for western Megalithism. From this point on it is possible to evaluate typological tendencies, to propose coherent chronologies that might explain decorative programs and to reflect on the ideology behind these records.

What does architecture tell us?

Archaeological evidences certify complex dynamics in monuments, which confirm previous processes. This data is visible through structures under tumuli, older material within more modern filling, and especially through the correlation with megalithic art that we propose to be essential to understand building sequences.

Structures under tumulus have been repeatedly pinpointed as the main context for the oldest Neolithic establishments. That agrees with patterns found within other Iberian areas where megaliths seem to materialise the first farmer's topographies. Data from Galicia certifies that deposits beneath the tumulus do have broader chronologies, and that the megaliths' building process was carried

ACTIVITY BENEATH OF THE BURIAL MOUNDS CONSTRUCTION				
SITE NAME	ARCHITECTURE	BIBLIOGRAPHY	EVENTS	CHRONOLOGIES
ILLADE 0 (As Pontes, A Coruña)	Barrow and chamber remains	Vaquero, 1999	Two ditches	5820±160 BP; 5059-4345 BC. (Beta-51901, IL0.80212) 5305±50 BP; 4314-3986 BC. (GrN-19208, IL0.55248) 5240±60 BP; 4228-3953 BC. (GrN-19210, IL0.80212)
ILLADE 1 (As Pontes, A Coruña)	Barrow and chamber remains	Vaquero, 1999	Pits of posts	2970±200 BP; 1406-926 BC. (GrN-19212, IL1.33372)
ILLADE 2 (As Pontes, A Coruña)	Barrow	Vaquero, 1999 & 1998-2005	Ditch	Copper Age - Bronze Age
CHAO DE REBOREDO 1 (As Pontes, A Coruña)	Barrow	Vaquero, 1995	Ditch	3820 ±70 BP; 2464-2034 BC. (GrN-19214, RB1.15679)
A GÁNDARA (Miño, A Coruña)	Barrow	Vilaseco, 2006; Fábregas & Vilaseco, 2013	Ditches of cabin	Beginning or final Tumular Phenomenon (2500 BC - 900 BC)
DOMBATE (Cabana de Bergantiños, A Coruña)	Barrow with polygonal chamber	Bello, 1992/93	A big tumulus covers his Radius and also the place Where an oldest chamber Had previously been built and dismantled	3940 - 3630 cal. BC.
CHOUSA VELLA (Cerceda, A Coruña)	Barrow	Vidal,2003	Diachrony between two ritual and funerary moments	No data
TÚMULO PA 28 DE LA SERRA DO BOCELO (Toques, A Coruña)	Barrow	Criado et al. 1991	Ditch in the substratum	No data
FORNO DOS MOUROS (Toques, A Coruña)	Barrow with polygonal Chamber and passage-graves	Criado et al. 1991; Steelman 2005.	Two diachronic construction phases	3800-3620 Cal BP
MADORRA DA GRANXA (Castro de Rei, Lugo)	Barrow with chamber	Chao & Álvarez, 2000	Ditches	Diachronic data
MEDORRAS 2 Y 3 DE ROZA DAS AVEAS (Outeiro de Rei, Lugo)	Two barrows with polygonal chambers	Prieto et al. 2010; Prieto & Vázquez 2011; Fábregas & Vilaseco, 2013	6 burning structures: 2 under de RA2; and 3 under the RA3; and 1 over the barrow RA3	Late Neolithic. 2500-2000 a.C
CHOUSA NOVA 1 (Silleda, Pontevedra)	Barrow with chamber	Domínguez-Bella & Bóveda 2011	Long ditches around the barrow and a possible quarry	5450 ± 40 BP; 4350-4240 Cal BC (Beta-277240)
MÁMOA DE ESPIÑEIRA (Boiro, A Coruña)	Barrow	Nodar, 2007	Longitudinal sections and pits of posts.	No data
MÁMOA 6 DE OS CAMPIÑOS (Rianxo, A Coruña)	Barrow with chamber	Fábregas & De La Fuente, 1991-1992; Fábregas & Vilaseco, 2011	Pits in the chamber area and 21 orifices (3 cm of diam. average)	Late Neolithic / Cooper Age Before the Bell Beaker Period Final of 4th - beginning of 3rd millenniums
TÚMULO DE SANTA CATALINA (Caldas de Reis, Pontevedra)	Barrow	Vidal, 2007	Ditches and burning structures	3rd Millennium
MÁMOA 1 DE AS ROZAS (Campo Lameiro, Pontevedra)	Barrow whit polygonal chamber	Patiño,1984b; Suárez et al. 1998	Fireplace under the tumulus	4th Millennium
CHAN DA CRUZ (Vilaboa, Pontevedra)	Barrow whit chamber	Patiño,1984a; Suárez et al. 1998	Fireplace under the tumulus	4th Millennium
MÁMOA DO REI (Vilaboa, Pontevedra)	Barrow with polygonal chamber and passage-graves	Castro & Vázquez, 2007	Diverse building phases, at least 3 floor phases are overlapped in the access	No data
COTOGRANDE 1 (Vigo, Pontevedra)	Barrow with chamber	Abad, 1992-93	Gradient reduction in the substratum	5230±80 BP (GrN-17689 CGr89)
COTOGRANDE 5 (Vigo, Pontevedra)	Barrow with chamber	Abad, 1995; Fábregas & Vilaseco, 2004; Fábregas & Vilaseco, 2011	Ditch	4065±45BP (GrN-19595 Coto Grande 3 A) 4390±50 BP (GrN-19595 Coto Grande 3 B)
TÚMULO DEL MONTE VIXIADOR (Vigo, Pontevedra)	Barrow with polygonal chamber with a possible and short passage-grave	Vázquez, 2007	Ditch	No data
OS CONSELLOS (Nigrán, Pontevedra)	Barrow with chamber	Cano, Vázquez & Vidal, 2000; Fábregas & Vilaseco 2004 and 2011	Burning structures and ditches	First half part of the 3rd millennium
EVIDENCES ON THE BURIAL MOUND MASS: FILLS WITH AN ANCIENT MATERIALS				
SITE NAME	ARCHITECTURE	BIBLIOGRAPHY	EVENTS	CHRONOLOGIES
A MILLARADA 1 (Cospeito, Lugo)	Tumulus with polygonal chamber	Vidal, 2001-2002	Oval pit over the burial mound mass	At the peak period of the megalithic monuments / burial mound development
ROZA DAS AVEAS (Outeiro de Rei, Lugo)	Tumulus with polygonal chamber opened	Prieto; Lantes, O; Vázquez, P & Martínez, 2010; Fábregas & Vilaseco, 2013	Intentional depositions on the surface of the burial mound mass	Early or peak period of the megalithic monuments / burial mound development. Between the end of the 5th Millennium and the beginning of the 4th Millennium beginning. Pottery fragments of the Neolithic Period -Penha type- or the Late Bronze Age
MADORRA DA GRANXA (Castro de Rei, Lugo)	Tumulus with chamber	Chao & Álvarez, 2000	Fills on the burial mound mass with a deposition of grey sediments	No data
MARCO DO CAMBALLÓN 5 (Vila de Cruces, Pontevedra)	Tumulus with chamber	Fábregas & de la Fuente, 1988; Fábregas & Vilaseco, 2013	on the surface of the burial mound mass & pits over the burial mound mass	1600–800 BC
MONTE ROMEÁ (Lalín, Pontevedra)	Tumulus with polygonal chamber	Mañana, 2003	Fills closuring the access structure	3366-3084 cal BC
OS CONSELLOS (Nigrán, Pontevedra)	Tumulus with chamber	Cano; Vázquez & Vidal, 2000	Recovered burial mound & fills on the burial mound mass	First half millennium

TABLE 1. ACTIVITY BENEATH THE BURIAL MOUNDS CONSTRUCTION AND EVIDENCES OF THE BURIAL MOUNDS MASS IN GALICIA'S MEGALITHS.

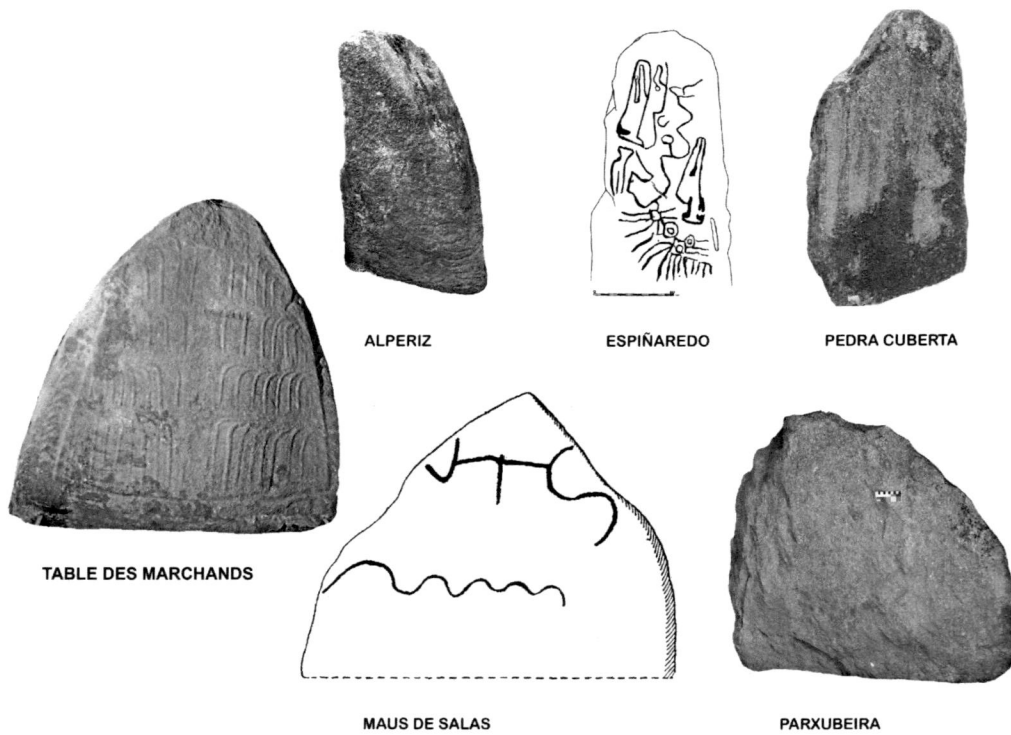

FIGURE 2. SOME EXAMPLES OF TRIANGULAR STELAE FOUND IN THE GALICIAN MEGALITHS' CONTEXT, AND TABLE DES MARCHANDS CHAMBER`S STELE.

out through various phases and not exclusively during 4th/5th millennia cal. BC, widely accepted timeframe for Iberian historiography.

Tumuli re-usage is less known although it is increasingly more significant considering that evidences have been found in other places within the Atlantic seaboard (Barroso *et al.* 2007). Some of the oldest Galician dates, sampled from the tumulus' mass, show the existence of a system with Atlantic reminiscences: the filling beneath the tumulus is composed of older materials. The tumulus of Mont Saint-Michel, whose filling was taken from a Mesolithic shelter located nearby the coast, is a most paradigmatic example.

Another novelty is the study of burial spaces' transformations and re-constructions (see the bibliography gathered for the tables), the most evident being the process of remaking the tumulus and the closures of the structure in differentiated moments (*vide Table 2*).

This whole succinct and not quite exhaustive picture aims to integrate the use and construction of these funerary spaces within the same complexity range as the one documented for the classic areas of the Atlantic megalithism, which Galicia had been artificially separated from. Taken into account its rich and diverse megalithic art as an obvious reference, diachrony is unquestionable for Galician megalithism.

What does parietal art tell us?

Advances in understanding the Galician megalithism graphic representations are influenced by two historiographical events that took place during the 90s: the work by Bello (1994) on diachronic

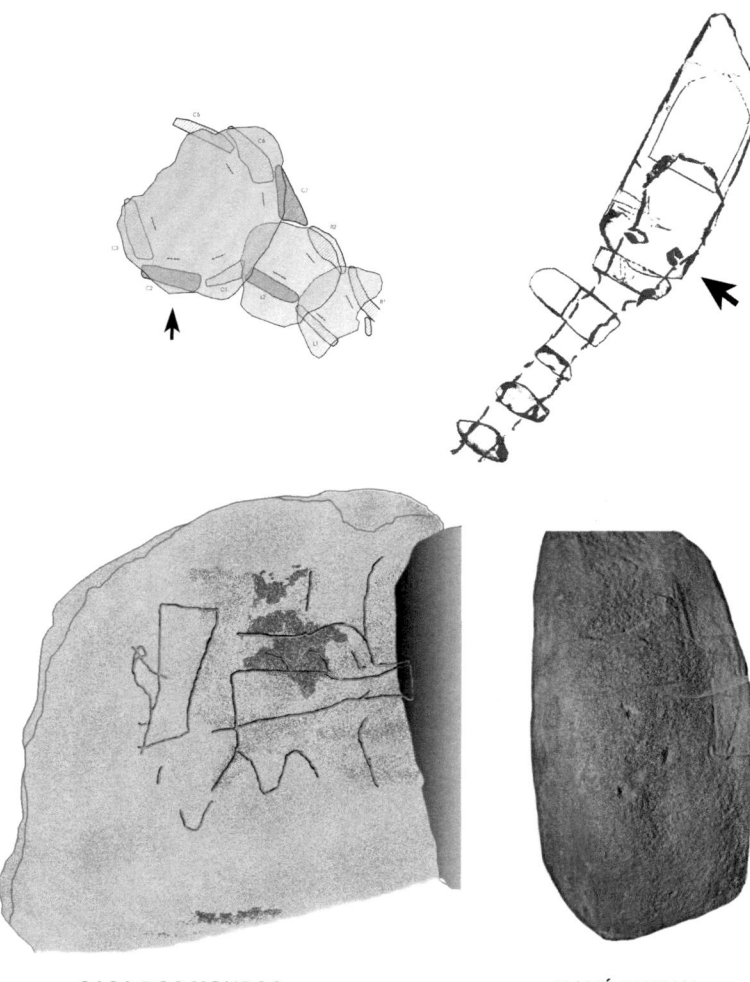

FIGURE 3. "THE THING" SEQUENCE. RED PAINT AND ENGRAVINGS IN *CASA DOS MOUROS* (GALICIA) AND *MANÉ RUTUAL* (BRITANY). IN BOTH SITES THE COVER SLAB IS ALSO AN ANTHROPOMORPHIC STELAE.

sequences in the dolmen of Dombate, where both the sculptural pieces found within the entrance area and the sequence "small monument-big monument" and uprights' decoration are useful to effectively analyse maintenance, use and remaking processes; secondly, Bradley's project on open-air art (Bradley *et al.* 1993).

These two lines of work have evolved independently. On one hand data about construction diachrony of megaliths is increasingly more abundant (Fábregas, Vilaseco 2013). On the other hand more evidences of the relationship between an open-air Atlantic-influenced art (Fábregas, Vilaseco 2008) and megalithic art, rather set aside in the past (Bueno *et al.* 2009), are being found. The existence of reused uprights in Galicia (Bueno *et al.* 2007 a; Carrera, 2011) is confirmed through a reassessment of the archaeological landscape.

One of the commonest forms of reused uprights is stelae placed at the monument's head or nearby. The front piece of *Table des Marchands* (Cassen, Robin, 2009) in Britanny constitutes a classic example to enunciate some common characteristics: the upright is sculpted differently, frequently with a pointed end, the outline is integrally worked, and occasionally engravings and paintings extend beyond the limits determined by adjacent pieces, either the cover slab or the trench where they rest.

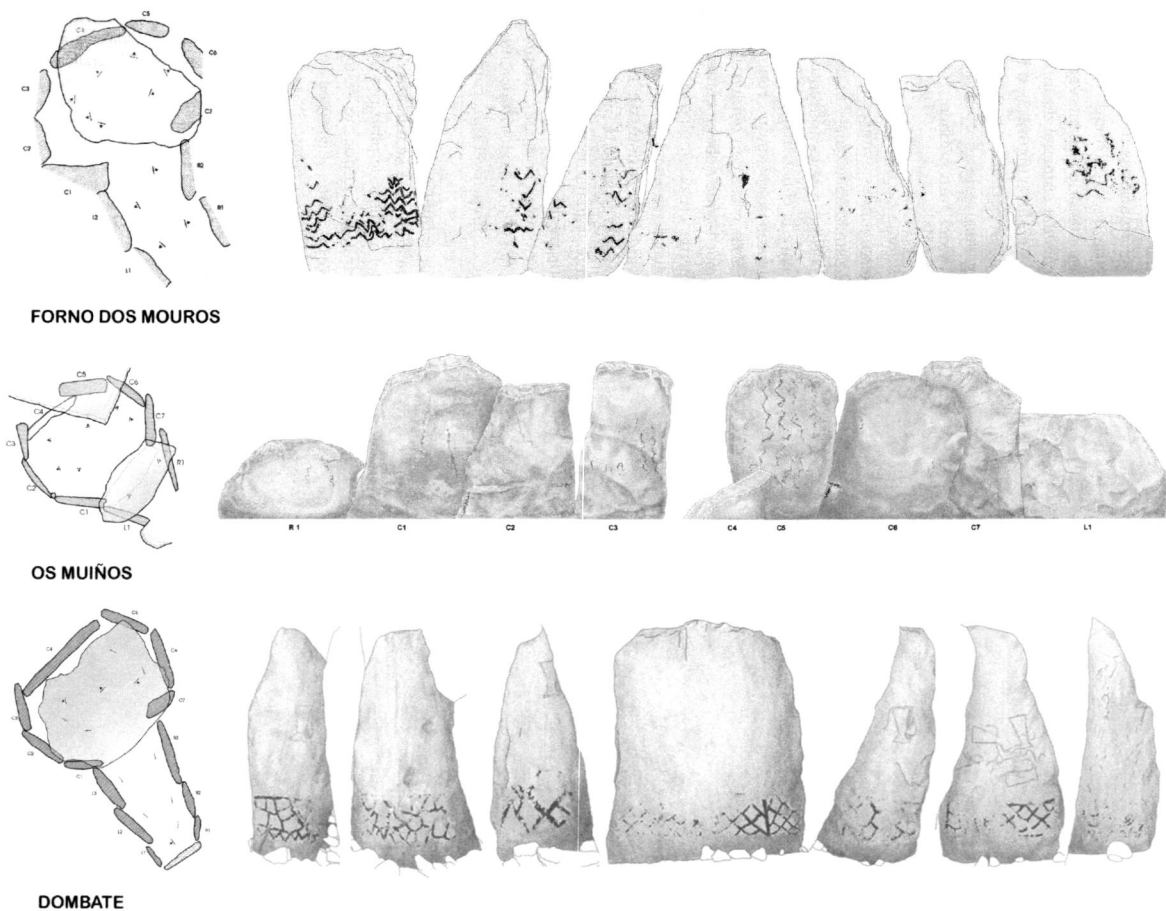

FIGURE 4. PLANS FROM *FORNO DOS MOUROS*, *OS MUIÑOS* AND *DOMBATE* SHOWING REUSED UPRIGHTS AND ANTHROPOMORPHIC COVER SLABS.

There is a remarkable abundance of this short of triangular stelae in Galicia: *Mámoa da Cruz* in Alperiz, *Parxubeira*, *Forno dos Mouros*, *Maus de Salas* 2, *Marco de Camballón* 1, *Anta do Serramo*, *Pedra Coberta* o *Espiñaredo* 11. All of them reiterate that triangular shape, where pigments and engravings certainly have a specific role. The stelae from *Anta do Serramo* is a painted piece that provided the oldest direct dating for pigments within the whole record of Iberian dolmens (Carrera, Fábregas 2002); the one from *Pedra Coberta*, another engraved stelae, was also directly dated (Steelman *et al.* 2005). Waves and engraved suns represent the oldest phase in the usage of the stelae from *Marco do Camballón* 1 (Carrera 2011: 457). That suggests the importance of wavy graphies, also visible in the stelae from *Maus de Salas* 2 and in the one from *Espiñaredo* 11 (Carrera 2001: 454). The latter also has circles with sticking-out spokes and possible weaponry (Shee, García 1973: 338). Thus stelae that were previous to the monuments were decorated using both paintings and engravings.

References for pointed shapes can also be found in open-air environments in regions like Brittany or the South-west. For instance the *Currás* menhir and the more obvious, given its proximity to the dolmen 1 of San Cibrao, triangular stelae-menhir found in Allariz, are noteworthy in Galicia (http://www.arqueomas.com/peninsula-iberica-megalitismo-dolmenes-de-sancibrian).

The slab from Tourón (Cabrejas *et al.* 2009) responds to well-known patterns of dolmenic uprights' re-usage as well. The way it has been sculpted and its angular engravings are quite similar in

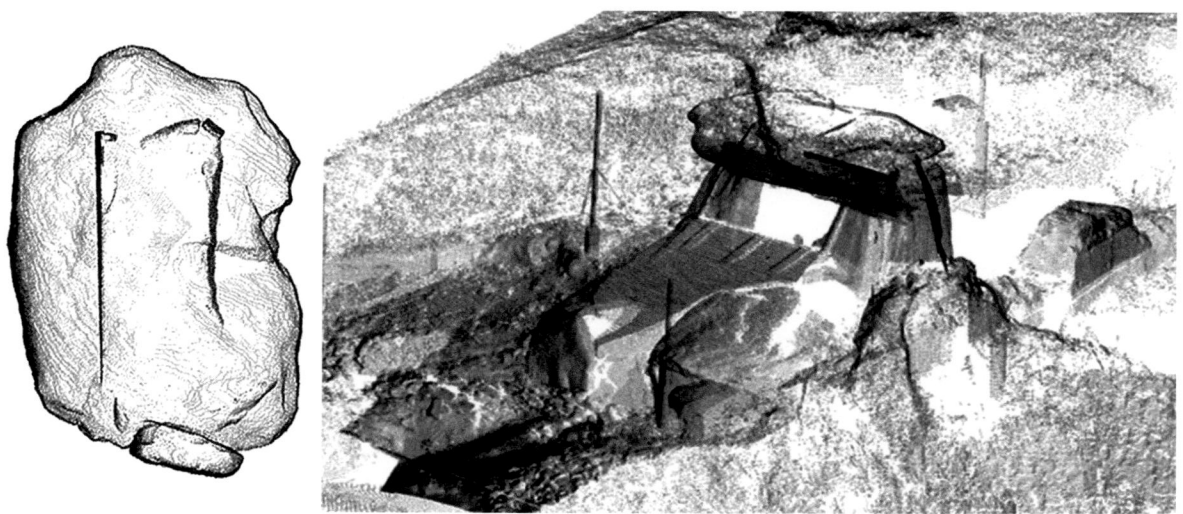

FIGURE 5. THE ANTHROPOMORPHIC STELAE FROM *DOMBATE*. ELEVATION.

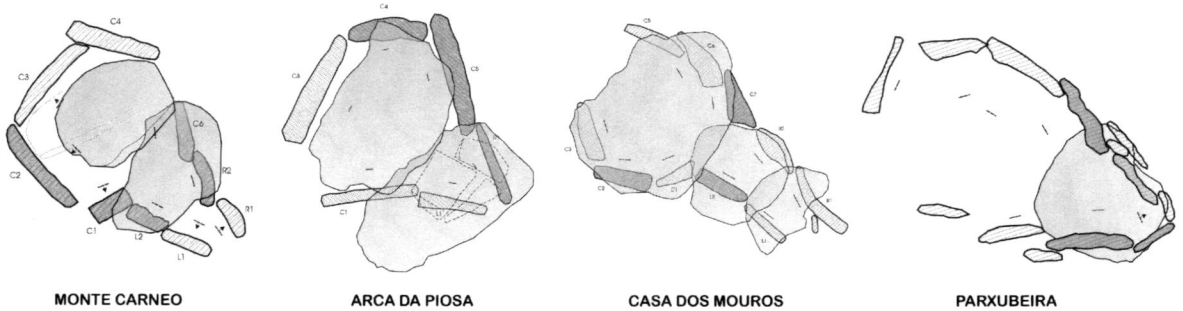

FIGURE 6. AN EXAMPLE OF SOME PLANS OF GALICIAN MEGALITHS THAT HAVE ANTHROPOMORPHIC COVERS.

technique and style to one of the uprights from Navalcán (Toledo) or to the better-known dolmen of *Chao Redondo* (north of Portugal).

Rectangular shapes that tend to define body volumes are rather frequent. The reused stelae of *Os Campiños* provides a contextual reference to the understanding of re-usage within other more southwestern areas (Bueno *et al.* 2011). An exhaustive review of decorated monuments would most likely result in more evidences, more than we have gathered here (*vide Table 2*). *Mámoa de Foxo*, still being analysed, has a reused stelae located at the front of the site's chamber: rectangular and with rounded edges in the superior part, two carved cavities play the role of eyes and clearly suggest that this is yet another humanized image.

There are no repeated graphies within the surface of the other uprights and they are sculpted from other kind of stone (Orthogneiss), because of that the slab C2 from *Casa dos Mouros* must be singled out. Given that it is a piece of granodiorite, C2 could only have been obtained from a source located

Public images, private readings: multi-perspective approaches to the post-Palaeolithic rock art

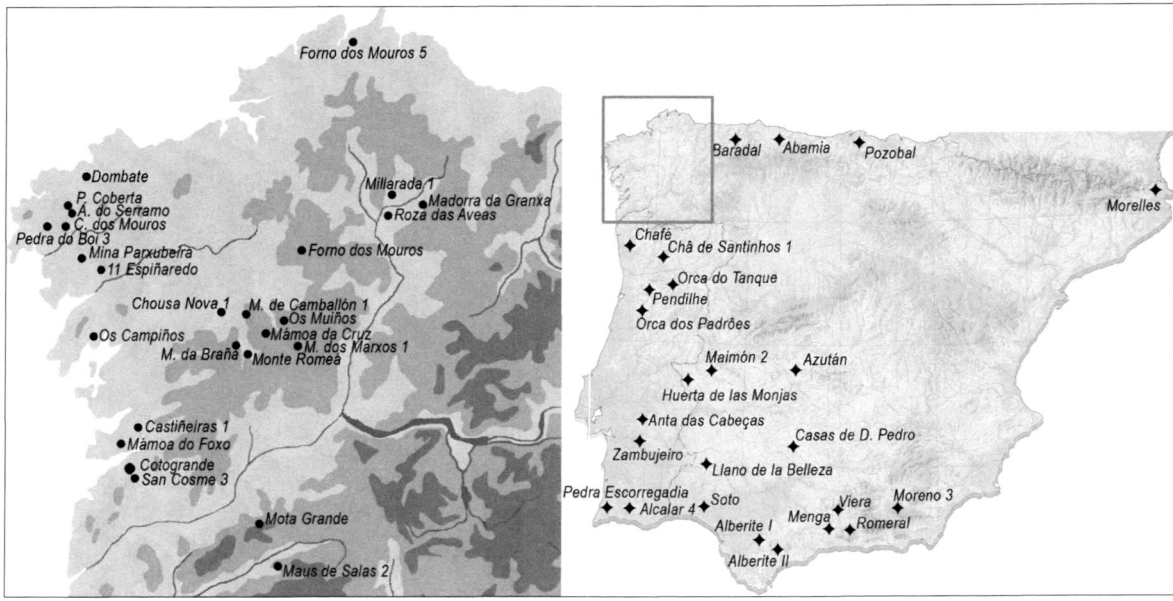

FIGURE 7. REUSED STELAE AND MENHIRS WITHIN THE IBERIAN PENINSULA (ELABORATED FROM BUENO *ET AL*. 2007) WITH GEOGRAPHIC DISPLAY OF TABLE 2 DATA.

10 km away from the current site (Carrera 2011: 311). This slab is the only one showing engravings ("The Thing"), which on the other hand repeat the same formula found in menhirs decorated in a similar way from *Mané Rutual* dolmen (Brittany). The engravings are covered by two overlapping layers of complex pigments (Carrera 2011: 315). The monument cover slabs are anthropomorphic.

Figures are lightly shaped by suggesting head, shoulders and waist. That is the case of some of the uprights in the dolmen of *Dombate*. From the frontal slab of the chamber (C4) to C1, C3, C5, and C6, all of them are associated to wavy engravings and the motive known as "The Thing". This setting has to be directly compared to the oldest phase of *Casa dos Mouros*. Some of the mentioned engravings are covered by other slabs; this confirms their reused nature. Each one of them has a continuous layer of complex pigment which equalises the monument's graphic program (Carrera 2011: 431). The whole panorama is even more appealing when the anthropomorphic cover slab is considered.

There are more examples of this process of complete reformulation of an ancient megalithic space in Galicia. Every upright in *Os Muiños* is silhouetted, with head and shoulders. A previous red-painted decoration ensures the relation between sculptural and painted elements. Above this first decorative phase, the surface was repainted in black and white after applying a plaster primer, and it has been directly dated (Carrera 2008: 123). The cover slab resting on the corridor uprights shows a stelae-like short of profile that suggests it should be integrated within the described old group. *Pedra Coberta*, already mentioned because of its triangular stelae, is constructed using older stelae as covers and uprights as well. Complex pigments in the site have been directly dated too.

As well as triangular shapes suggest humanized figures in the dolmen context, some menhirs found in open-air sites can also be defined as anthropomorphic shapes. That is the case of the menhirs of *Cristal* (Villoch 1998) and the one from *Gargantáns*. The latter has an undulated engraved form which can be interpreted as a snake covering the whole surface (Bueno, Balbín 1995).

SITE NAME	ARCHITECTURE	BIBLIOGRAPHY	EVENTS		CHRONOLOGIES
			EVIDENCES OF THE EXTENSION PHASES ON THE MOUND	STELES & MENHIRS REUSED	
FORNO DOS MOUROS 5 (Ortigueira, A Coruña)	Tumulus with polygonal chamber	Mañana, 2005	The tumular filler cover the destroyed chamber, as well as a previous chamber and a tumulus. Also, there is a new filler in the access of the destroyed chamber.		4552-4351 cal. BC 4410-4306 cal. BC
DOMBATE (Cabana, A Coruña)	Tumulus with polygonal chamber	Bello, 1993	Two sequences of tumular filler construction	Reutilised stele all the chamber and the cover	3715-3635 cal. BC (tumulus)
PEDRA COBERTA (Vimianzo, A Coruña)	Tumulus with polygonal chamber	Carrera, 2011		Possible reutilised steles all the chamber and the cover	3960-3690 cal BC (paintings)
ANTA DO SERRAMO (Vimianzo, A Coruña)	Tumulus with polygonal chamber	Carrera, 2011		Possible Reutilised stele	5300-4700 cal BC (paintings)
CASA DOS MOUROS (Vimianzo, A Coruña)	Tumulus with polygonal chamber	Carrera, 2011		Reutilised stele C2	
PEDRA DO BOI 3 (Dumbría, A Coruña)	Tumulus with "chamber"	Lestón, 2009	The destruction of the old camera, the expansion of the tumular filler for the construction of a circular structure in its centre and rear covering.		
A MINA PARXUBEIRA M2 (Mazaricos, A Coruña)	Tumulus with polygonal chamber	Rodríguez, 1998		Possible Reutilised stele	
MAMOA 11 Espiñaredo (Negreira, A Coruña)	Tumulus with indetermined chamber	Shee & García, 1973		Possible Reutilised stele	
FORNO DOS MOUROS (Toques, A Coruña)	Tumulus with polygonal chamber	Criado et al. 1991		Possible Reutilised stele	
TÚMULO 1 DE A MILLARADA (Cospeito, Lugo)	Tumulus with poligonal simple chamber	Vidal, 2001-2002.	Tumulus completely rebuilt.	Chamber with a possible anthropomorphic orthostat	
MADORRA DA GRANXA (Castro de Rei, Lugo)	Tumulus with chamber	Chao & Álvarez, 2000		Possible anthropomorphic orthostat	
ROZA DAS AVEAS (Outeiro de Rei, Lugo)	Tumulus with polygonal chamber opened	Fábregas & Vilaseco, 2013		Slab vertical displacement and later reuse	Final 5th Millennium cal BC/ beginning of the IV cal BC
CHOUSA NOVA 1 (Silleda, Pontevedra)	Tumulus with chamber	Domínguez-Bella & Bóveda, 2011	Two sequences of tumular filler construction		4350-4240 Cal BC
MARCO DE CAMBALLÓN 1 (Vila de Cruces, Pontevedra)	Tumulus with polygonal chamber	Carrera, 2011		Possible Reutilised stele	
MÁMOA DOS MUIÑOS (A Golada, Pontevedra)	Tumulus with chamber	Carrera, 2008		Reutilised stele all the chamber and the cover	3640-3550 Cal BC 3540-3370 cal BC (paintings)
MÁMOA DA CRUZ (Lalín, Pontevedra)	Tumulus with indetermined chamber	Sobrino & Martínez, 1958		Possible Reutilised stele	
MONTE DOS MARXOS 1 (Rodeiro, Pontevedra)	Tumulus with indetermined chamber	Carrera, 2011		Possible Reutilised stele	
MÁMOA DA BRAÑA (Silleda, Pontevedra)	Tumulus with polygonal chamber	Carballo & Vázquez, 1984		Possible Reutilised stele	
TÚMULO DE MONTE ROMEÁ (Lalín, Pontevedra)	Tumulus with polygonal chamber	Mañana, 2003	Two sequences of tumular filler construction		3962-3756 cal BC 3366-3084 cal BC
CASTIÑEIRAS 1 (Vilaboa, Pontevedra)	Tumulus with polygonal chamber	Castro & Vázquez, 2007	Tumulus completely rebuilt.	Reutilised stele C1	
MÁMOA DO FOXO (Moaña, Pontevedra)	Tumulus with polygonal chamber	Unpublished		Possible Reutilised stele	
TÚMULO DE COTOGRANDE 1 (Vigo, Pontevedra)	Tumulus with chamber	Abad, 1992-93	Enlargement of the filler tumulus over the peristalith.		5230 ± 80 BP
TÚMULO DE COTOGRANDE 5 (Vigo, Pontevedra)	Tumulus with chamber	Abad, 1995		A set of slabs, accumulated in the tumulus	4065±45BP 4390± 50BP
TUMULO 3 ALTO DE SAN COSME (Mos, Pontevedra)	Tumulus with an stele in his centre	Parcero, 1998.	Two sequences of tumular filler construction		
MOTA GRANDE (Verea, Ourense)	Tumulus with polygonal chamber	Chao, 2000	Tumulus completely rebuilt.	Reutilised stele all the chamber	
MAUS DE SALAS 2 (Muiños, Ourense)	Tumulus with indetermined chamber	Fortes, 1901		Possible Reutilised stele	

TABLE 2. EVIDENCES OF THE EXTENSION PHASES ON THE MOUNDS AND STELAE AND MENHIRS REEMPLOYED IN GALICIA'S MEGALITHS.

Megalithic art and the monument's biography

Reused stelae and menhirs confirm previous roles and reinforce the interest of analysing the monument's biography through each slab's history. These sequences offer two very interesting options for interpretation in Galicia. Firstly, the mentioned archaeological evidences, the pre-existing structures found beneath the tumulus, are an indication of events that happened before building the monuments. Old stelae and menhirs could be linked to this first stage and could have been the very reason for the beginning of the construction. This possibility becomes far more significant when considering that there is evidence for abandoned tumuli with small monuments inside that were built over with bigger structures that reused older slabs and stelae. Dombate is a paradigmatic example, and *Forno dos Mouros* is probably too. There are more cases of potential previous structures. Singles stelae and anthropomorphic front uprights add up to graphic programs with engravings and paintings, and all together they form a data set that reflects building phases and usage stages. Related to this hypothesis the following sites have to be considered: *Pedra Coberta, Monte dos Marxos, Parxubeira, Os Muiños, Casa dos Mouros* and *Anta do Serramo*. Detecting anthropomorphic cover slabs is the key to this approach, which does not differ from well-known Atlantic Megalithism interpretations.

Some classic examples clearly illustrate our point. *Mané Rutual*, which has fragmented and decorated ("The Thing" engravings) pieces of menhirs and red paintings, as we have been able to demonstrate recently, also possesses an enormous anthropomorphic cover slab. The archaeological record from the dolmen of *Berceau* is a helpful aid to understand moving and relocating sequences of certain pieces in tumuli that have two natures: an old one and a new one. The first monument was dismantled and a new one was then built right next to the former. Both sepulchres' tumuli were rebuilt afterwards. The cover slab from the first monument, that has head and shoulders, was probably erected between both structures, showing its value as a visible anthropomorphic reference. It was then located as the cover of the second monument. Human bone remains have been dated around the second half of the 5th millennium cal. BC (Jagu 2003).

Anthropomorphic slabs in Galician dolmens add to those detected in the north of Portugal: *Os Padroes* and *Orca do Tanque*. Those detected in the Cantabrian area, the already mentioned ones in Catalonia (Bueno *et al.* 2007a, 2009) and the better-known ones in the south-west (Bueno *et al.* 2013), are equally significant and constitute a good reference to state the broad spread of the old stone's usage as the foundation for most Iberian dolmens.

There is another yet unpublished argument that will add to the evaluation so these sequences. By studying the painted decoration, it is feasible to read chronologies and to define maintenance phases including engravings. The complex sequence painting-engraving found in *Dombate* and *Casa dos Mouros* completes the archaeological record and confirms a rather deep re-executing process which implies and specific symbolic program. Studies on painting-engraving superposition in the Northwest strongly suggest that analysed events are far more extensive in time (Carrera 2001: 50). The hypothesis of long-term remaking of monuments, otherwise observed with difficulty – archaeological and manufacture evidences seem to be less indicative – is quite appealing, although if applied generally it should be treated with precaution.

The existence of more than one recognisable technique may respond to an individual action or there may be a temporal hiatus of unknown length. Both in northern Portugal and in Galicia the link between simple paintings and engravings is particularly frequent: while some sites (*Cunha Baixa, Barrosa*) are uncertain, there is an evident contemporary relation (*Eireira, Cimo de Vila*) or even complementarity (*Picoto do Vasco, Chã de Arcas V, Portela do Pão, Juncal* and *Anta do Meixueiro*) in others. In *Madorras* and *Castiñeiras I* engravings are previous to simple paintings. The latter also has some clearly trimmed (shaped head) uprights that could have been used before the construction of the current chamber. This monument was intensively rebuilt (Castro and Vázquez 2007). The engraved sign on the C1 slab repeats the already-understood first phase of *Os Muiños*. Furthermore,

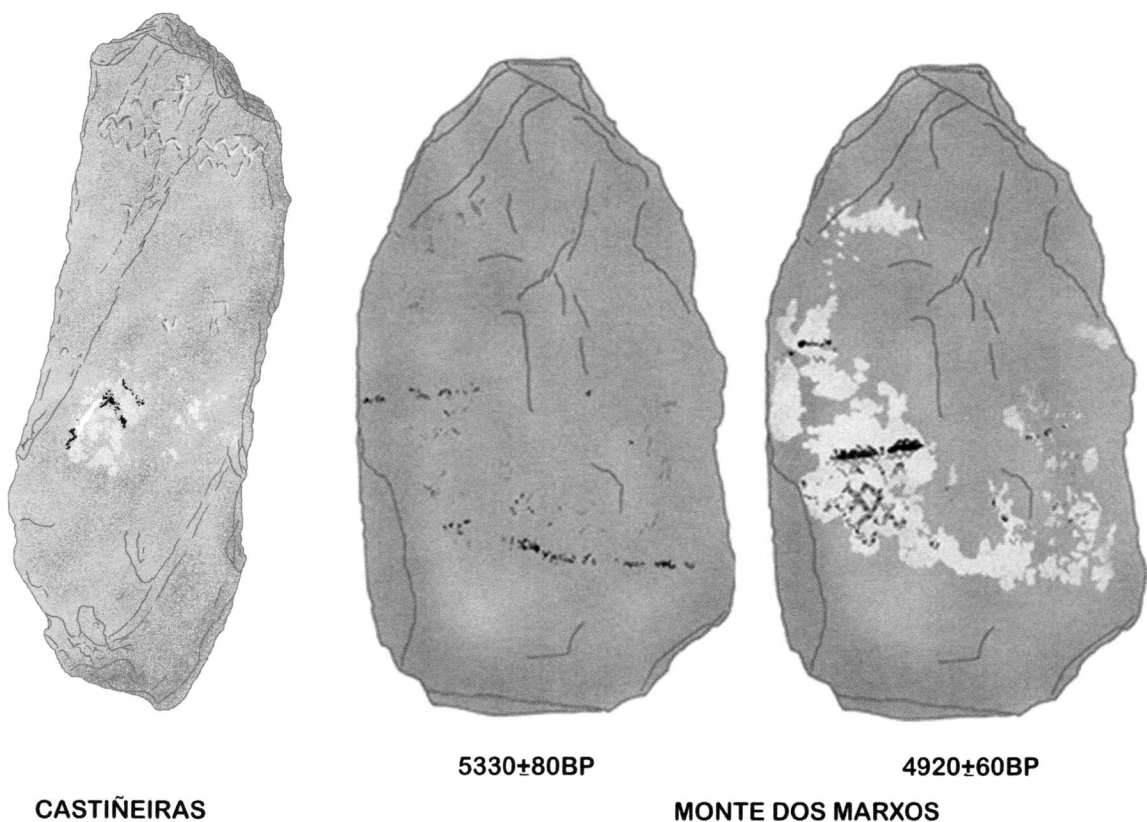

FIGURE 8. REUSED UPRIGHTS WITH TECHNIC SEQUENCES: STELAE FROM *CASTIÑEIRAS* (ENGRAVINGS AND PIGMENTS) AND STELAE OF *MONTE DOS MARXOS* (SIMPLE AND COMPLEX PAINTING) WITH C14 DATES OF THE TWO PIGMENT PHASES.

it is a new reference to support the idea that *Castiñeiras* was built from previously-used stelae, similar to those found in *Os Muiños*.

As they are from the different moments, complex painting superpositions over engravings (occasionally repainted more than once) found in *Dombate* and *Casa dos Mouros* are of more importance. Superposition is obvious in some sites (*Fojo*, Portugal) and thus sometimes (for instance in *Monte dos Marxos*) engraving, simple paintings and complex painting superposition is visible. The two repainted layers have a rather considerable time lapse between each other: 4380-3980 and 3810-3630 cal. BC, respectively (Carrera 2011: 444). Therefore it is not surprising that some uprights show anthropomorphic features.

Finally, there are other examples of more than two stages superposition that will have to be analysed in the future. The best documented cases are in the north of Portugal: *Anta de Antelas* and *Anta de Aliviada*. Both sites show a vertical stratigraphy of simple painting, complex painting and engravings, where the latter seems to have eliminated previous paintings (Shee 1974). Another singular example is *Mota Grande*, a monument, probably rebuilt at some point (Chao 2000), where every single technique is present (engraving, sometimes accompanied with paint, and complex painting). Nearby *Mota Grande*, *Portela do Pão* (Baptista 1997: 209) has very superficial *piqueté* over a black primer. We relate this to the paleolithic scraping technique and we consider its presence inside the H chamber of *Barnenez* (France) to be remarkably interesting (Bueno *et al.* 2015).

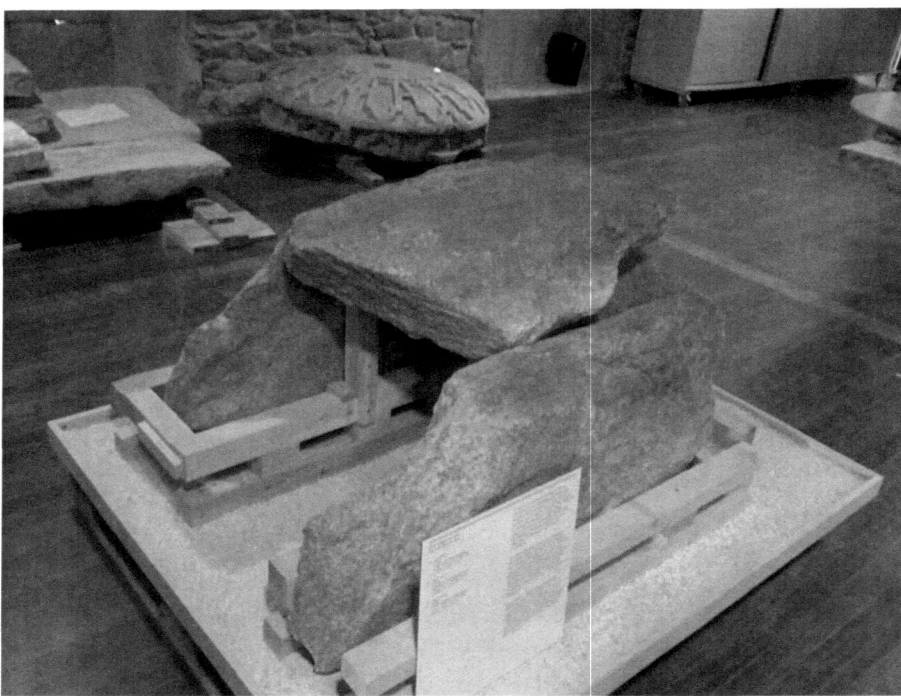

FIGURE 9. *BICO DE LAGOS* CIST. MUSEO DAS MAREAS. A CORUÑA.

Megalithic art and diachrony in the northwest Iberian area monuments

The superposition of techniques provides an unprecedented argument to the study of megaliths' diachrony, not only for early phases but also for the different maintenance and remaking processes. Therefore an exhaustive analysis of the megalithic graphic programmes is a turning point in the possible implementation of this kind of methodology within the European context (Bueno *et al.* 2014). Evidences of activity under tumuli add up to previous slabs' re-usage to place a whole set of ritual expressions within an specific time frame: the late 4th and early 5th millennium cal. BC. Furthermore, that links megalith builders' ideas to the first signs of agriculture, including the reaffirmation of ancient topographies (Bueno *et al.* 2007b).

Galicia provides archaeological and graphic data of notable importance to support our approach. That construction phase where old stelae and menhirs are the foundation of the megaliths is supported in Galicia by the direct chronologies of the uprights from *Anta do Serramo*, *Monte dos Marxos*, *Pedra Coberta* and *Dombate*. They provide a date *postquem* that confirms that between the end of the 5th and the beginning of the 4th millennium cal. BC these processes are quite extended. There are comparable and acceptable chronologies for similar events in Brittany. The role of "The Thing" in previous stelae and menhirs is visible in *Dombate* and *Casa dos Mouros*, and both sites have strong enough evidences to confirm the mentioned time frame. Wavy and sun-like engravings increase the graphical spectrum linking it to Iberian Schematic Art.

The continuity of building new monuments over older ones is an evidence of long diachrony, as it has been corroborated by III millennium archaeological contexts in Galicia (Bradley 2004; Vázquez 1980; Villar 2012). More recently, the stelae related to *Devesa do Rei*'s foundation trench (Aboal *et al.* 2005) suggests a very close link to the painted megalithic stelae from Corte Campo II, which was found in a late Bronze trench and we consider to be a reused piece (Ramos 2007; Bueno *et al.* 2009).

The evidence of engraving that could be related to petroglyphs in the upper side of some cover slabs adds a new element to the discussion. Such is the case with *Peña Tú*-like symbol on the cover of the dolmen of *Pendilhe* (Bueno *et al.* 2007a). If it had been covered by the tumulus, the engravings should have been inserted in the same temporal phase of the monument usage. The petroglyph fragment found inside the filling of a dolmen's tumulus in Monte Pirleo is a remarkable reference for this hypothesis (García Martínez 1975). However if these engravings were out in the open, the monuments' cover would have signified the same short of symbology that can be read on the open-air panels. The above-described slabs have a particular interest taking into account that they were used to cover the ancestors' deposits. This interpretation agrees with the hypothesis supporting the relevant value of anthropomorphic shapes in open-air panels (Bueno *et al.* 2005).

Considering decorated megaliths, menhirs and petroglyphs, and the hypothesis of a diachrony between the late 4th and early 5th millennium cal. BC, the quantitative index of graphic evidences is highly pronounced in Galicia. Such a level of singificance is only found in a few emblematic places of the Atlantic Megalithism record.

Given the current state of knowledge, Megalithism in Galicia consolidates the presence of old stelae and menhirs, evidences of transformations and continuous rebuilding of monuments, and human-images exhibitions in open areas or in the burial sites' entrance, as system thoroughly used to give a ritual value to the ancestors' graves. The ideology expressed by these ritual expressions multiplies the applicable approaches for the study of a social framework that supports the process of megaliths building around Europe.

Acknowledgement

This work utilises the results of ongoing projects: HAR2012-34709, HAR2015-68595-P and 10SEC530009PR. We are very much obliged for the helpful aid of the Xunta de Galicia in letting us go through unpublished reports. The original text has been translated from Spanish by Álvaro de Balbín Bueno and Sara Prieto Huecas.

Bibliography

ABAD GALLEGO, X. C. 1993. Balance de las actuaciones arqueológicas llevadas a cabo en la necrópolis megalítica de Cotogrande (Cabral): Campañas de 1989-1992. Castrelos 5-6: 7-28.

ABOAL, R.; AYÁN, X. M.; CRIADO, F.; PRIETO, M. P.; TABARÉS, M. 2005. Yacimientos sin estratigrafía: Devesa do Rei, ¿un sitio cultual de la Prehistoria Reciente y la Protohistoria de Galicia?. *Trabajos de Prehistoria*, 62-2, pp. 165-180.

BAPTISTA, A. M. 1997. Arte megalítica no planalto de Castro Laboreiro (Melgaço, Portugal e Ourense, Galiza). Brigantium, 10. pp. 191-216.

BELLO, J. M. 1993. El monumento de Dombate en el marco del megalitismo del noroeste peninsular. Aspectos arquitectónicos. *Portugalia, Nova Série*, XIII-XIV. pp. 139-148.

BELLO DIEGUEZ, J. M. 1994. Grabados, pinturas e ídolos de Dombate ¿grupo de Viseu o grupo noroccidental? Aspectos taxonómicos y cronológicos. Actas do Seminario O Megalitismo no centro de Portugal. Mangualde 1992. Centro de Estudios Prehistóricos da Beira Alta, pp. 287-304.

BARROSO, R.; BUENO, P.; CAMINO, J.; BALBÍN, R. DE 2007. Fuentenegroso (Asturias), un enterramiento del Bronce Final-Hierro en el marco de las comunidades atlánticas peninsulares. Pyrenae, Barcelona, nº 38, vol. 2. 2007: 7-32.

BLAS CORTINA, M. A. DE 1997. El arte megalítico en el territorio cantábrico: un fenómeno entre la nitidez y la ambigüedad.III Congreso Internacional de Arte megalítico. *Brigantium* 10, pp. 69-89.

BRADLEY, R., 2004. Os megalitos e as pedras decoradas da Grâ-Bretanha e Irlanda no contexto europeu. Sinais de Pedra. Evora CD.

BRADLEY, R.; CRIADO, F.; FÁBREGAS, R. 1993. Rock art research as landscape archaeology a pilot study in Galicia, north-west Spain. *World Archaeology*, 25 (3). Londres.

BUENO, P.; BALBÍN, R. DE 1992. L'Art mégalithique dans la Péninsule Ibérique. Une vue d'ensemble. *L'Anthropologie*. Paris. 96, p. 499-572.

BUENO, P.; BALBÍN, R. DE 1995. La graphie du serpent dans la culture mégalithique péninsulaire: représentations a plein air et représentations mégalithiques. L'Anthropologie. Paris. T. 99. 1995, N°2/3, pp. 357-381.

BUENO, P.; BALBÍN, R. DE 2006. Between power and mythology: evidence of social inequality and hierarchisation in the Iberian Megalithic. In Díaz del Río, P., García Sanjuán, L. eds. – *Social Inequality in Iberian Late Prehistory*. BAR International Series 1525, p. 37-52.

BUENO, P.; BALBIN, R. DE; BARROSO, R. 2005. Hierarchisation et métallurgie: statues-armés dans la Péninsule Ibérique. L'Anthropologie 109, pp. 577-640.

BUENO, P.; BALBIN, R. DE; BARROSO, R. 2007a. Chronologie de l'art Mégalithique ibérique: C14 et contextes archéologiques. *L'Anthropologie*. Paris. 111, p. 590-654.

BUENO, P.; BALBIN, R. DE; BARROSO, R. 2007b. Ideología de los primeros agricultores en el Sur de Europa: las más antiguas cronologías del arte megalítico ibérico. *Cuadernos de Arte Rupestre* 4, p. 281-312.

BUENO, P.; BALBIN, R. DE; BARROSO, R. 2008. Dioses y antepasados que salen de las piedras. *Boletín del Instituto andaluz del Patrimonio Histórico*. 67, p. 62-67.

BUENO, P.; BALBIN, R. DE; BARROSO, R. 2012. La Frontera ideológica: grafias postglaciares ibéricas. Mesa Redonda I – Artes Rupestres da Pré-História e da Proto-História: Paradigmas e Metodologías de Registo. (Vila Nova de Foz Côa- Nov. 2010). Trabalhos de Arqueología. 54, p. 139-160.

BUENO, P.; BALBIN, R. DE; BARROSO, R. 2013. Símbolos para los vivos, símbolos para los muertos. Arte megalítico en Andalucía. In Martínez García, J. ed. *Arte Esquemático. Actas del II Congreso de Los Velez*, p. 25-47.

BUENO, P.; BALBIN, R. DE; BARROSO, R. 2014. Megalithic art in the Iberian Peninsula. Thinking about graphic discourses in the European Megaliths. *Préhistoire mediterranéen*, Colloque: Fonctions, utilisations et représentations de l'espace dans les sépultures monumentales du Néolithique européen. URL: http://pm.revues.org/1077. 22p.

BUENO, P.; BALBIN, R. DE; BARROSO, R.; CERRILLO, E.; GONZALEZ, A.; PRADA, A. 2011. Megaliths and stelae in the Inner Basin of Tagus river: Santiago de Alcántara, Alconétar and Cañamero (Cáceres, Spain). In Bueno, P.; Cerrillo, E.; Gonzalez, A. ed. – *From the Origins: The Prehistory of the Inner Tagus Region*. Oxford, BAR International Series 2219, p. 143-160.

BUENO, P.; BALBIN, R. DE; BARROSO, R.; LOPEZ QUINTANA, J. C.; GUENAGA, A. 2009a. Frontières et art mégalithique. Une perspective depuis le monde pyrenéen. *L'Anthropologie*. Paris. 113, p. 882-929.

CABREJAS, E.; MAÑANA, P.; SEOANE, Y. 2009. Achado dunhas lousas con arte megalítico en Fonte Tourón (Lalín, Pontevedra). Cuadernos de Estudios Gallegos, LV, N° 122, enero-diciembre, pp. 9-31.

CANO, J.; VÁZQUEZ, P.; VIDAL, M. A. 2000. La arquitectura del túmulo de Os Consellos (Nigrán, Pontevedra). 3° Congresso de Arqueología Peninsular, V. 3, Neolitizaçao e megalitismo da Península Ibérica. Jorge, V. O. (coord.): 337-356.

CRIADO, F.; BONILLA, A.; CERQUERINO, D.; DÍAZ, M.; GONZÁLEZ, M.; INFANTE, F.; MÉNDEZ, F.; PENEDO, R.; RODRÍGUEZ, E.; VAQUERO, J. 1991. El área Bocelo-Furelos. Entre los tiempos paleolíticos y medievales (Campañas de 1987, 1988 y 1989). Xunta de Galicia: 294.

CARRERA RAMÍREZ, F. 1997. Recientes aportaciones al catálogo de dólmenes pintados de Galicia. *Brigantium*, 10, A Coruña. pp. 409-414.

CARRERA RAMÍREZ, F. 2008. El dolmen de Os Muiños (Agolada, Pontevedra): intervención para la documentación y protección de la pintura megalítica conservada. Gallaecia, N° 27, 2008, pp. 113-135.

CARRERA RAMÍREZ, F. 2011. *El arte parietal en monumentos megalíticos del Noroeste Ibérico*. BAR International Series 2190, Oxford.

CARRERA, F. and FÁBREGAS, R. 2002. Datación radiocarbónica de pinturas megalíticas del Noroeste Peninsular. *Trabajos de Prehistoria* 59 (1). Madrid. pp. 157-166.

CARRERA, F. and FÁBREGAS, R. 2008. El estudio científico de los megalitos (2). *PH* 67. Monográfico Patrimonio Megalítico. Instituto Andaluz de Patrimonio Histórico. Sevilla. pp. 78-83.

CARRERA, F.; FÁBREGAS, R.; BELLO, J. M.; BALBÍN, R.; BUENO, P.; AYORA. 2005. Procedimiento interdisciplinar de caracterización, diagnosis y preservación de pintura megalítica. In: *Actas del II Congreso del GEIIC "Investigación en Conservación y Restauración"*. Barcelona, 9-11 November. 2005. pp. 30-40.

CASSEN, S.; ROBIN, G. 2009. Le corpus des signes à la Table des Marchands. In S. Cassen (dir.) Autour de la Table. Exploration archéologiques et discours savants sur des architectures néolithiques à Locmariaquer, Morbihan (Table des Marchands et Grand Menhir). CNRS. Université de Nantes, pp. 826-853.

CHAO, F. J.; ALVAREZ, I. A. 2000. A Madorra da Granxa: ¿O túmulo máis grande de Galicia?. Brigantium, 12, pp. 411-64.

CHAO ÁLVAREZ, F. J. 2000. Intervención arqueológica en A Mota Grande: aproximación a su arquitectura. Brigantium: Boletín do Museu Arqueolóxico e Histórico da Coruña, Nº 12, 2000, pp. 23-40.

DOMÍNGUEZ-BELLA, S.; BÓVEDA, Mª. J. 2011. Variscita y ámbar en el Neolítico gallego. Análisis arqueométrico del collar del túmulo 1 de Chousa Nova, Silleda (Pontevedra, España). Trabajos de Prehistoria, 68, Nº 2: 369-380.

FÁBREGAS, R; DE LA FUENTE, F. 1992. Excavación da Mámoa 6 de Os Campiños (Leiro, Rianxo). Campaña de 1984. Brigantium, 7: 91-149.

FÁBREGAS, R; VILASECO, I. 2004. El megalitismo gallego a inicios del siglo XXI. Mainake, 26: 62-87.

FÁBREGAS, R.; VILASECO, J. I. 2008. El Neolítico y el Megalitismo en Galicia: problemas teórico-metodológicos y estado de la cuestión "en VVAA: Muita gente poucas antas? Origens, Espaços e Contextos do Megalitismo. Actas do II Colóquio Internacional sobre Megalitismo. Brigantium 19: 281-304.

FÁBREGAS, R; VILASECO, I. 2011. Manifestaciones funerarias entre el III y II milenios a.C. en el Noroeste ibérico. Las comunidades campaniformes en Galicia: cambios sociales en el III y II milenios BC en el NW de la Península Ibérica. Prieto, Mª. P. y Salanova, L. (coord.). Diputación de Pontevedra: 231-240.

FÁBREGAS, R.; VILASECO, I. 2013. From west to west: the many lives of the Galician mounds. Tara-from the past to the future. Towards a new research agenda. Section 6 Perspectives and comparisons from overseas. O'Sullivan, M.; Scarre, Ch.; Doyle, M. (eds.). Dublin: 502-514.

FORTES, J. 1901. A necrópolis dolménica de Salles (Terras de Barroso). Portugalia, I. pp. 665-686.

GARCÍA MARTÍNEZ, M. C. 1975. Datos para una cronología del arte rupestre gallego. Boletín del Seminario de Estudios de Arte y Arqueología, XL-XLI: 477-500. Facultad de Letras de la Universidad de Valladolid.

JAGU, D. 2003. Une double condamnation à Changé, Saint-Piat (Eure et Loir). Révue Archéologique de Picardie, n° spécial, 21, pp. 147-155.

LAPORTE, L. 2010. Restauration, reconstruction, appropriation; évolution des architectures mégalithiques dans l'Ouest de la France, entre passé et présent". In *Actas del Congreso Internacional sobre Megalitismo y otras manifestaciones funerarias, contemporáneas en su contexto social, económico y cultural* (Beasain 2007). Munibe Suplemento 32, p. 120-150.

LESTÓN GÓMEZ, M. 2009. Escavación das mámoas de Prado do Rei e Pedra do Boi, Dumbría. Actuacións singulares Atlas arqueolóxico da comarca de Fisterra. Xunta de Galicia. Santiago de Compostela. 35-37.

MAÑANA BORRAZÁS, P. 2005. Túmulo 5 de Forno dos Mouros (Ortigueira, A Coruña). Primeiros resultados. Cuadernos de Estudios Gallegos, Tomo LII, Fasc. 118, Santiago. 39-79.

NODAR NODAR, C. 2007. Proxecto de sondaxes arqueolóxicas avaliativas e escavación na mámoa de Espiñeira, Boiro (A Coruña). Actuacións Arqueolóxicas: ano 2007. Xunta de Galicia: 226.

PRIETO, Mª. P.; LANTES, O.; VÁZQUEZ, P.; MARTÍNEZ, A. 2010. La cerámica de dos túmulos de Roza das Aveas (Outeiro de Rei, Lugo): un estudio diacrónico del estilo y la composición. Boletín del Seminario de Estudios de Arte y Arqueología, 76: 27-62.

RAMOS AGUIRRE, M. 2007. Cortecampo II (Los Arcos) y Osaleta (Lorca, Valle de Yerri). Sepulturas descubiertas en las obras de la Autovía del Camino. *La Tierra te sea leve. Arqueología de la muerte en Navarra,* Pamplona, pp. 93-96.

PARCERO OUBIÑA, C. 1998. La Arqueología en la gasificación de Galicia 3: excavación del Túmulo nº 3 del Alto de San Cosme. TAPA 5. CSIC: 35.

SHEE TWOHIG, E.; GARCIA MARTINEZ, M. C. 1973. Tres tumbas megalíticas decoradas en Galicia. Trabajos de Prehistoria, 30. pp. 335-348.

STEELMAN, K.; CARRERA, F.; FÁBREGAS, R.; GILDERSON, T. and ROWE, M. W. 2005. Direct radiocarbon dating of megalithic paints from north-west Iberia. *Antiquity*, Vol. 79, London. pp. 379-389.

VAQUERO LASTRES, J. 1999. Les extrêmes distincts. La configuration de l'espace dans les societés ayant bâti des tertres funéraires dans le Nord-Ouest ibérique. BAR Internacional Series 821. pp. 212. Oxford.

VAQUERO LASTRES, J. 1995. Túmulos tardíos en el NW. RB1: estructuras. Actas del XXII Congreso Nacional de Arqueología. Vigo. T.I: 405-410.

VÁZQUEZ COLLAZO, S. 2007. Intervención arqueolóxica no túmulo do Monte Vixiador, Candeán, Vigo (Pontevedra). Actuacións arqueolóxicas: ano 2007. Xunta de Galicia: 47-48.

VÁZQUEZ VARELA, J. M. 1980. "Enterramientos en cista de la Edad del Bronce en Galicia", *Pontevedra,* O, pp. 23-40.

VILASECO VÁZQUEZ, X. I. 2006. Á beira da morte. Algúns exemplos europeos sobre a utilización do contorno inmediato aos monumentos megalíticos funerarios como posíbeis modelos para Galicia. Gallaecia 25: 7-44.

VIDAL LOJO, M. Á. 2002. Excavación arqueolóxica no túmulo 1 de A Millarada (Cospeito). Boletín do Museo Provincial de Lugo, 10: 9-34.

VIDAL LOJO, M. 2003. Informe Valorativo. Excavación arqueológica del Túmulo nº 2 de Chousa Vella (Cerceda, A Coruña).

VIDAL LOJO, M. Á. 2007. Escavación arqueolóxica no novo túmulo de Santa Catalina e contorno próximo (Caldas de Reis, Pontevedra). Actuacións arqueolóxicas: ano 2007. Xunta de Galicia: 228-229.

VILLAR QUINTEIRO, R. 2012. Nueva necrópolis de la prehistoria reciente en Ribadetea. Ponteareas. Pontevedra. Gallaecia, 31:63-81.

VILLOCH VÁZQUEZ, V. 1998. Un nuevo menhir en Cristal. Gallaecia, 17: 107-19. Santiago de Compostela.

Illustrating the Sabor Valley (Trás-os-Montes, Portugal): rock art and its long-term diachrony since the Upper Palaeolithic until the Iron Age

Sofia Soares de FIGUEIREDO
Lab2PT-Landscapes, Heritage and Territory Laboratory. University of Minho, Portugal.
ACE, ODEBRECHT/Bento Pedroso Constructions and Lena Engineering –
Estaleiro do Baixo Sabor
sofia.csf@gmail.com

Pedro XAVIER, Dário NEVES, José MACIEL
ACE, ODEBRECHT/Bento Pedroso Constructions and Lena Engineering –
Estaleiro do Baixo Sabor

Luís NOBRE, Isabel DOMÍNGUEZ GARCÍA
ACE, ODEBRECHT/Bento Pedroso Constructions and Lena Engineering –
Estaleiro do Baixo Sabor
ACINEP- Prehistory Studies Institute; Environment and Culture Study Centre

Abstract

The construction of a major dam in the Trás-os-Montes region of Northeast Portugal, has led to an unprecedented archaeological survey that included a specific study of rock art over an area of 3000 hectares. Over the past four years, the implementation and development of this study revealed that the number of rock art sites is much higher than initially expected. In addition, the quality and the chronologies of the findings are exceptional, not only in a regional context but on a peninsular and European scales.

The present paper seeks to explore a specific geographical area within the Sabor Valley, where we found the highest concentration of rock art sites, with chronologies ranging between the Upper Palaeolithic to the Contemporary Period. However, this paper will only focus on the rock art produced between the Upper Palaeolithic and the Iron Age.

From the Palaeolithic era, we will look at the Foz do Medal terrace and its collection of exceptional portable art with over 1500 engraved fragments. Regarding rock art from the transition of the Holocene and post-Palaeolithic period, we will focus our attention on three main sites containing original depictions of caprids and cervids. Finally, we will look at Iron Age plaques uncovered in the Crestelos site. We would like to stress the fact that all mentioned sites are located within an area of less than 2 kilometers.

Due to the concentrated materiality in a very restricted area, our aim is to approach different continuities and discontinuities in terms of rock art archaeological records. Were the same animals depicted in the Upper Palaeolithic as in the post-Palaeolithic periods? Why do we find mobile supports both in the Palaeolithic and Iron Age periods and none in the time in between? These are some of the questions that will be addressing.

Key words: *Rock art; Palaeolithic; recent Pre-History; Iron Age; Northeast Portugal*

Rèsumè

La construction d'un barrage de grande ampleur en Trás-os-Montes, région du Nord-Ouest du Portugal, a conduit à une recherche archéologique sans précédent dans laquelle s'est insérée une étude spécifique de l'art rupestre s'étendant sur une surface de 3000 hectares. Au cours des quatre dernières années, l'implantation et le développement de cette étude ont révélé que les sites d'art rupestre été beaucoup plus nombreux que ceux initialement prévus. En outre, la qualité et les chronologies des découvertes sont exceptionnelles, non seulement à l'échelle régionale comme à l'échelle péninsulaire et Européenne.

Cet article vise à explorer une zone géographique spécifique dans la vallée du Sabor, dans laquelle nous avons trouvé une grande concentration de sites d'art rupestre, avec des chronologies allant entre le Paléolithique supérieur et la période contemporaine.

Cependant, cet article ira se concentrer uniquement sur l'art rupestre produit entre le Paléolithique supérieur et l'Âge du Fer.

En ce qui concerne l'ère Paléolithique, nous nous pencherons sur la terrasse du Foz du Medal et sa collection d'art mobilier exceptionnel ayant plus de 1500 fragments gravés.

Pour ce qui est de l'art rupestre, de la transition entre de la période Holocène et la période post-Paléolithique, nous focaliserons notre attention sur trois principaux sites contenant des représentations originales de caprinés et de cervidés. Pour terminer, nous nous pencherons sur les plaquettes de l'Âge du Fer découvertes dans le site de Crestelos. Nous tenons à insister sur le fait que tous les sites mentionnés sont situés sur une étendue de moins de deux kilomètres.

En raison de la concentration de matériel dans un espace unique et limité, notre objectif est d'aborder différentes continuités et discontinuités en matière de registres d'art rupestre. Est-ce que se sont les mêmes animaux qui ont été représentés au Paléolithique supérieur comme dans les périodes post- paléolithiques? Pourquoi trouvons-nous des supports mobiles à la fois dans les périodes Paléolithique et à l'Âge du Fer et aucun entre ces deux ères. Ce sont quelques-unes des questions que nous aborderons.

Mots clés: *Art rupestre; Paléolithique; Préhistoire Récente; Âge du Fer; Nord-Ouest du Portugal*

1. Introduction

The Trás-os-Montes region is located in the very Northeast of Portugal and until very recently it was an unexplored area in terms of its archaeological potential. The lack of large academic projects conducting archaeological field work in this area, as well as the regions poor quality infrastructure, kept away most archaeologists and researchers, who concentrated in other points of the country, known to be more prolific in archaeological findings.

Fortunately, just across the Douro River that limits this region to the South, the well-known Côa valley opened a precedent through a great discovery that drew the attention of whole world. In the Côa valley, more than one thousand engraved rocks on which Palaeolithic motifs stand out for their splendour, made UNESCO to classify this region as World Heritage in 1998. Due to this amazing discovery and its consequences, new institutes of archaeology were created and re-organized, and the so-called preventive or rescue archaeology grew and became completely professionalised.

In the beginning of the twenty first century, major constructions were planned for the Trás-os-Montes region. One of these constructions, the Baixo Sabor hydroelectric project, had a huge impact on the landscape, and submerged an area of 3000 hectares. In order to minimize the impacts, a Plan for Heritage Protection[1] was created, which began in 2010, and is now coming to an end.

The study of rock art in the Sabor valley begun in 2010 and, at that time, the plan was to study around 30 rock art sites. However, in the following 4 years, deep field surveys were conducted all over the valley, and, by the end of 2013, the number of rock art sites had grown to the astonishing number of around 200 (totalizing open air and shelters), 700 decorated blocks from different modern and contemporary constructions, and more than 2000 plaques from different archaeological excavations. During 2014, a huge database was under construction, taking into account more than 10,000 motifs discovered in the Sabor valley river, and distributed on different supports and with chronologies ranging from the Upper Palaeolithic until the contemporary period. With only 4 years of fieldwork and 1 year to process this huge mass of information, it should be easy to understand that the study and understanding of the rock art found in the Sabor valley is an immense work still being undertaken.

---

[1] The Plan of Heritage Protection is part of the Baixo Sabor Hydroelectric Exploitation, promoted by EDP Production, and whose implementation is the responsibility of Baixo Sabor, ACE- ODEBRECHT/Bento Pedroso Constructions and Lena Engineering. The Plan of Heritage Protection has the following structure of coordination: General Coordination: Paulo Dordio; Research coordinators: Filipe Santos (Cilhades), José Sastre (Protohistory), Luis Fontes (Middle Ages), Paulo Dordio (Modern and Contemporary Periods), Rita Gaspar (Prehistory), Sérgio Antunes (Monitoring), Sérgio Pereira (Romanization), Sofia Soares de Figueiredo (Rock Art), Susana Lainho (Conservation). The Plan of Heritage Protection is part of the Environment, Quality and Safety Area coordinated by Augusta Fernandes.

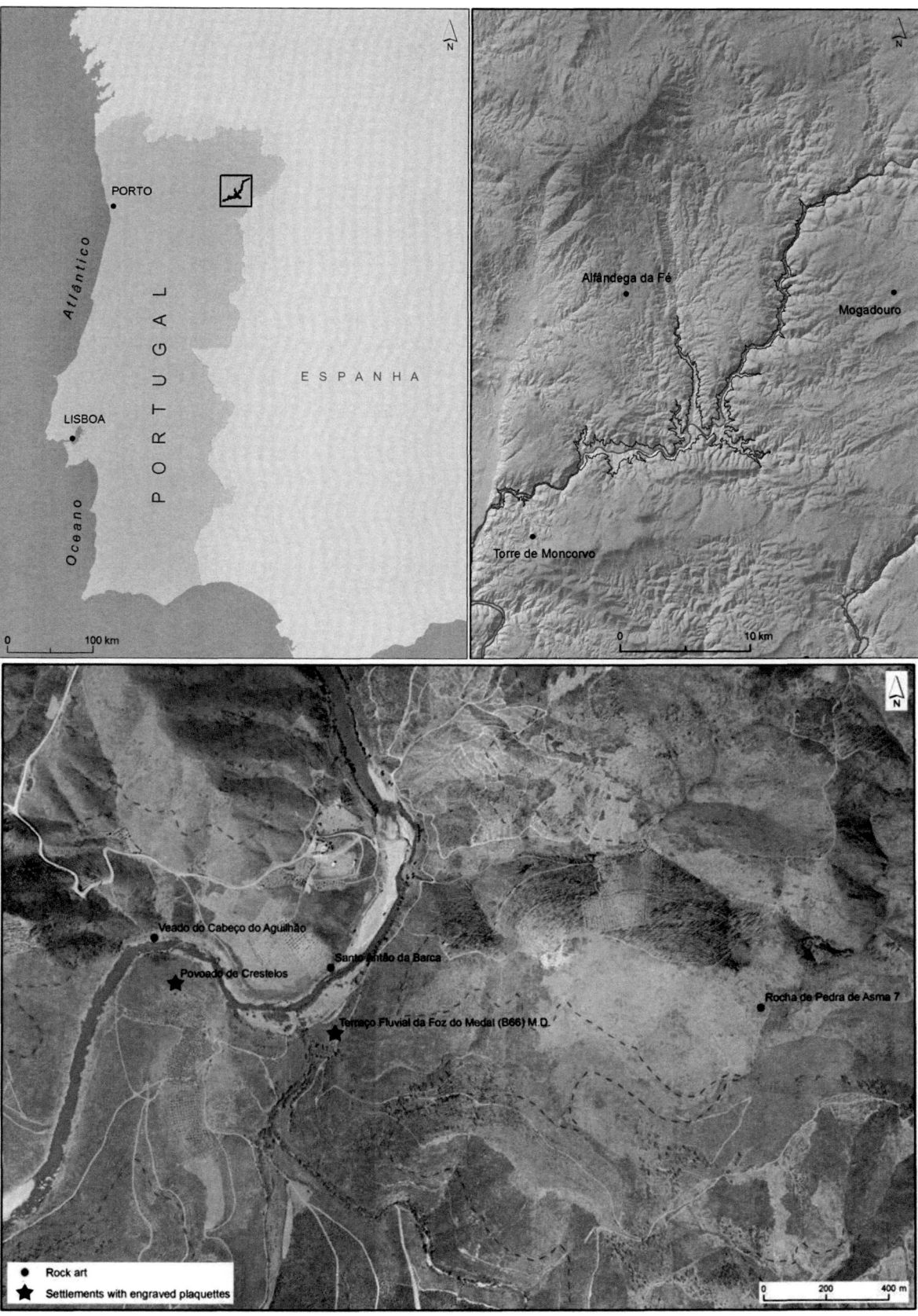

FIGURE 1. LOCALIZATION OF THE ARCHAEOLOGICAL SITES MENTIONED IN THE TEXT, IN THE SABOR VALLEY AND PORTUGUESE CONTEXT. MAP BY JOÃO MONTEIRO.

Looking at the Sabor River (Figure 1), we can easily observe that it is a deep valley, with V shaped slopes, although, in some areas, it opens up into more wide spaces. It is precisely in these areas, where streams are found and passageways become easier, that we find concentrations of human occupation (Figueiredo, Nobre *et al.* 2014:13).

2. Palaeolithic Art and the Foz do Medal Terrace

The excavation of the Medal river terrace started in 2011 and, one of the most amazing findings was the layer 1055. The total number of plaques found in the right bank of the Foz do Medal Terrace is 1504, although we are still studying the data related to the different layers, making this number a preliminary one. As the layer 1055 is the best understood up to present, in this text we will focus only on the engraved plaques from this deposit. Nevertheless, in our large scale thematic analysis conducted in this article, all the figurative motifs from the Foz do Medal terrace will be taken into account.

Although the integrity of the collection was maintained, layer 1055 has suffered a post-depositional relocation, leading all the materials to be found in a secondary context (Figueiredo, Nobre *et al.* 2014:14; Figueiredo, Nobre *et al.*, in press: 435). Taking into account the stratigraphic position of this layer, as well as the characteristics of the lithic assemblage recovered, we are dealing with Palaeolithic art from the Magdalenian period.

The collection is difficult to characterize due to the fragmentation of the pieces, and this created a great amount of work trying to reassembly as many fragments as possible. As a result, 254 fragments were reassembled into 170 complete or semi-complete plaques (Figueiredo, Nobre *et al.*, in press: 441). Still, the collection is very fragmented, and to recognise the represented motifs in the majority of plaques fragments is very difficult if not impossible. Nevertheless, the plaques on which we were able to identify the depicted motifs show us amazing figures, typical from the local Palaeolithic repertoire, with some original features (Figure 2).

The raw material used was mostly greywacke and schist, and about 170 plaques are engraved in both surfaces. We were able to identify three main techniques in the engraving of the slabs: fine, superficial engraving; deep engraving; and, in a residual number, a picking technique.

Concerning the figurative themes represented in increasing order of appearance, we can recognize goats, horses, aurochs and *cervids*. At least one anthropomorphic figure was also identified in the figurative themes. It is rather interesting to notice that most represented figures are the ones that display a higher technical variability in their execution, being the best example represented by the *caprids*. Also in terms of style, we were able to distinguish two different trends, one more schematic, the other more natural one. However, different styles do not necessarily correspond to different chronologies and, our first impressions led us to the assumption that they were contemporary. Nevertheless, future studies focusing mainly the recognized overlaps can show otherwise.

3. Art from the Holocene transition and recent Pre-History

Moving further in, and following a chronological sequence, we will now leave the Foz do Medal Terrace behind and continue to the open air rock art manifestations of the Holocene transition and recent Pre-History. In order to do so we have to move towards the east, climbing gentle slopes that lead us to a small valley formed by a tributary stream of the Medal stream or creek, where we find the first of the three analysed sites.

However, before we get there, it should be stressed that the three outcrops we aim to analyse in this section, have already been object of publication in two different works. The first constitutes the PhD thesis of the first author (Figueiredo, 2013) of this article and, the second, is a paper that has been accepted to be published in the Conference Proceedings of the III International Meeting

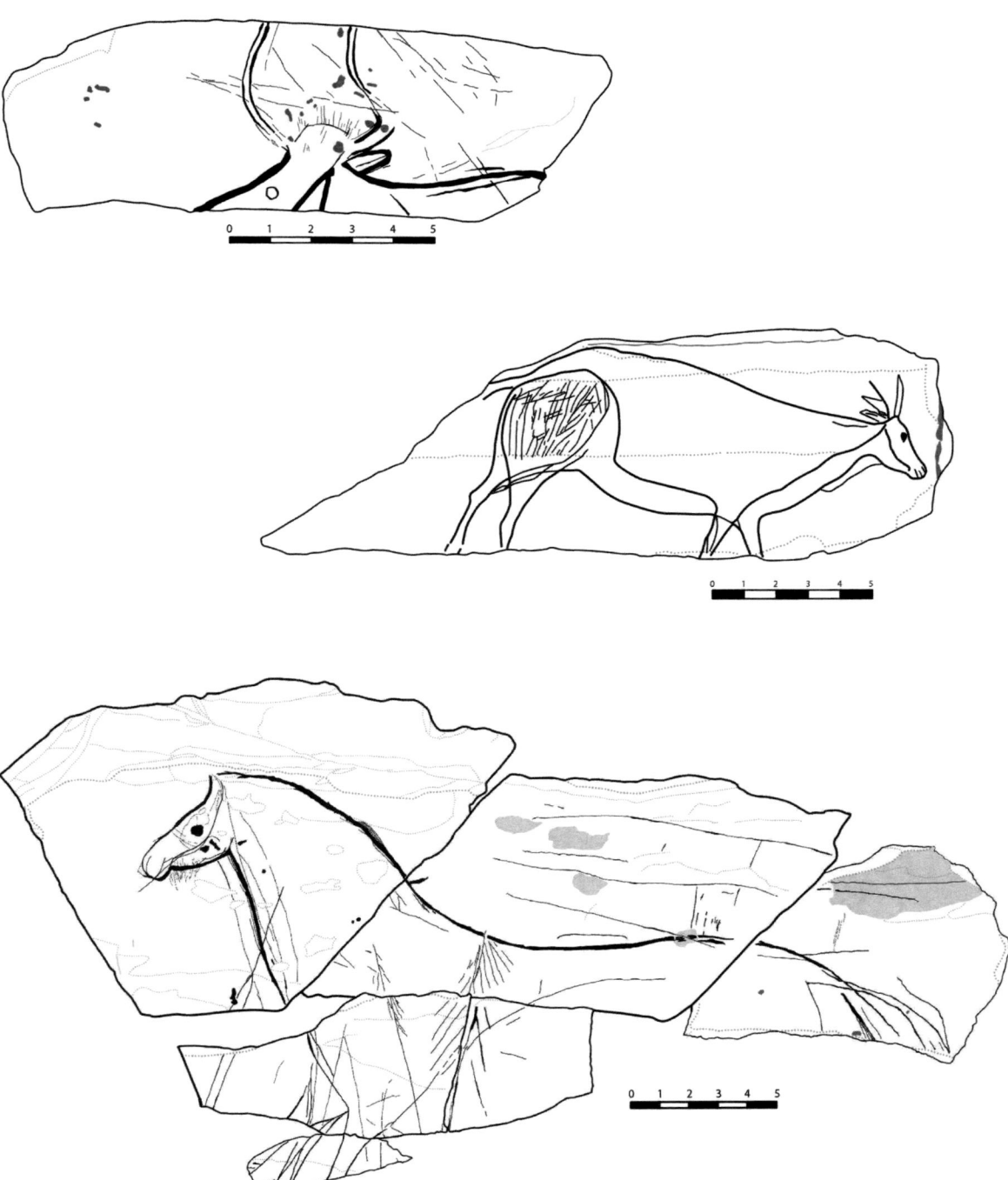

FIGURE 2. ENGRAVED PLAQUES FROM THE FOZ DO MEDAL TERRACE WITH REPRESENTATION OF AN AUROCH, AN IBEX AND A HORSE. ACCORDING TO FIGUEIREDO, NOBRE *ET AL.* 2014, IN PRESS.

of Doctorates and Post doctorates: Art in Prehistoric Societies, held in Nerja in 2013 (Figueiredo, Xavier *et al.*, in press). In this sense we will sum up the main ideas already presented in the mentioned papers.

In the small valley formed by the tributary stream of the Medal, the Ribeira da Pedra de Asma stream, on the right bank we find one of the most surprising rocks of the Sabor Valley. This rock is organized into three engraved panels. We will only approach Panel A and its earliest chronology, as the remaining motifs are from historical periods. In this panel are eight motifs that refer to a group of lines presenting different directions. In the middle of these series of lines we detected a zoomorphic figure that represents a small *caprid* (Figure 3). In terms of analogies, it is interesting to notice that this is the first figure to be found in the Trás-os-Montes area presenting these stylistic features: a less natural formalism, new shapes and silhouettes and greater predominance of the multiple traced incision (e.g. Baptista, 2009). In both Foz Côa and Siega Verde areas these designs correspond to the transition between the Palaeolithic and the Post-Palaeolithic periods.

Going down the stream again, towards the west, we find another rock art site called Santo Antão da Barca where we have identified five zoomorphic drawings associated with diverse picking and dimple techniques, representing deer. One of these figures stands out due to the concentration of its picked elements around the inner part of the body, which generate a sense of prominent volume, and, therefore, in our interpretation, suggest a pregnant female. Males seem to be absent from this group, which is interpreted as the representation of a matriarchal group (Figure 3). Considering the natural cycles of this specimen, and that the births occur between May and June, we may conclude that the figurines are representing the springtime season (Figueiredo, Xavier *et al*., in press: 197).

Further downstream, on the same bank, we find the third open-air rock art site considered in this section, named "Veado do Cabeço do Aguilhão" rock. Here we find the representation of a male deer facing upstream, and looking towards the rock we have just described. The representation leaves no doubt that we are dealing with a male given the size of the antlers, the tail represented facing upwards and the stretched neck, suggest the rutting period, which occurs between October and December (Figure 3).

The proximity of both rocks from the course of the river is responsible for their natural submersion in certain periods. Under these circumstances, we believe that a real dynamic between these two rocks and the waters was created: subsequent to the deer's mating season (represented by the Veado do Cabeço do Aguilhão rock), the river level rises and begins to decrease in the springtime, when the new-borns come- represented by the Santo Antão da Barca rock.

Trying to ascribe chronologies to these two rocks is difficult, since they are unique in the Trás-os-Montes region and their best parallels are to be found not in the Côa Valley, but in the Tagus Valley. Our proposals locate these motifs somewhere between the Neolithic and the Chalcolithic, although we assume that this large time span can become even larger in the light of new data that we are currently processing.

4. Iron Age rock art and the Crestelos settlement

If we stand on the Veado do Cabeço do Aguilhão rock and look to the other side of the Sabor River, we see a high hill with an imposing appearance. This hill is one of the two excavated areas where Iron Age remains were identified. In fact, concerning the Iron Age period, the so-called Crestelos area can be divided into two different spaces: an area on the top of the hill, where structures for storage were found; and another area at the foothill, where the settlement was located (Sastre, 2014:79). In the same area but from later chronologies, remains of a Roman settlement were also found as well as constructions dating from historical times.

In the Crestelos archaeological site, 105 engraved plaques were found. 32 engraved plaques were found at the foot of the hill, mainly decontextualized due to their later use in the construction of structures, and 73 were found at the top of the hill. Also at the top of the hill the excavation revealed five rock outcrops with Iron Age engravings. In Castelinho, another Iron Age settlement only 7 kilometres downstream from Crestelos, these artefacts were also found totalizing an impressive number of 521 engraved plaques (e.g. Santos, Sastre *et al*. 2012).

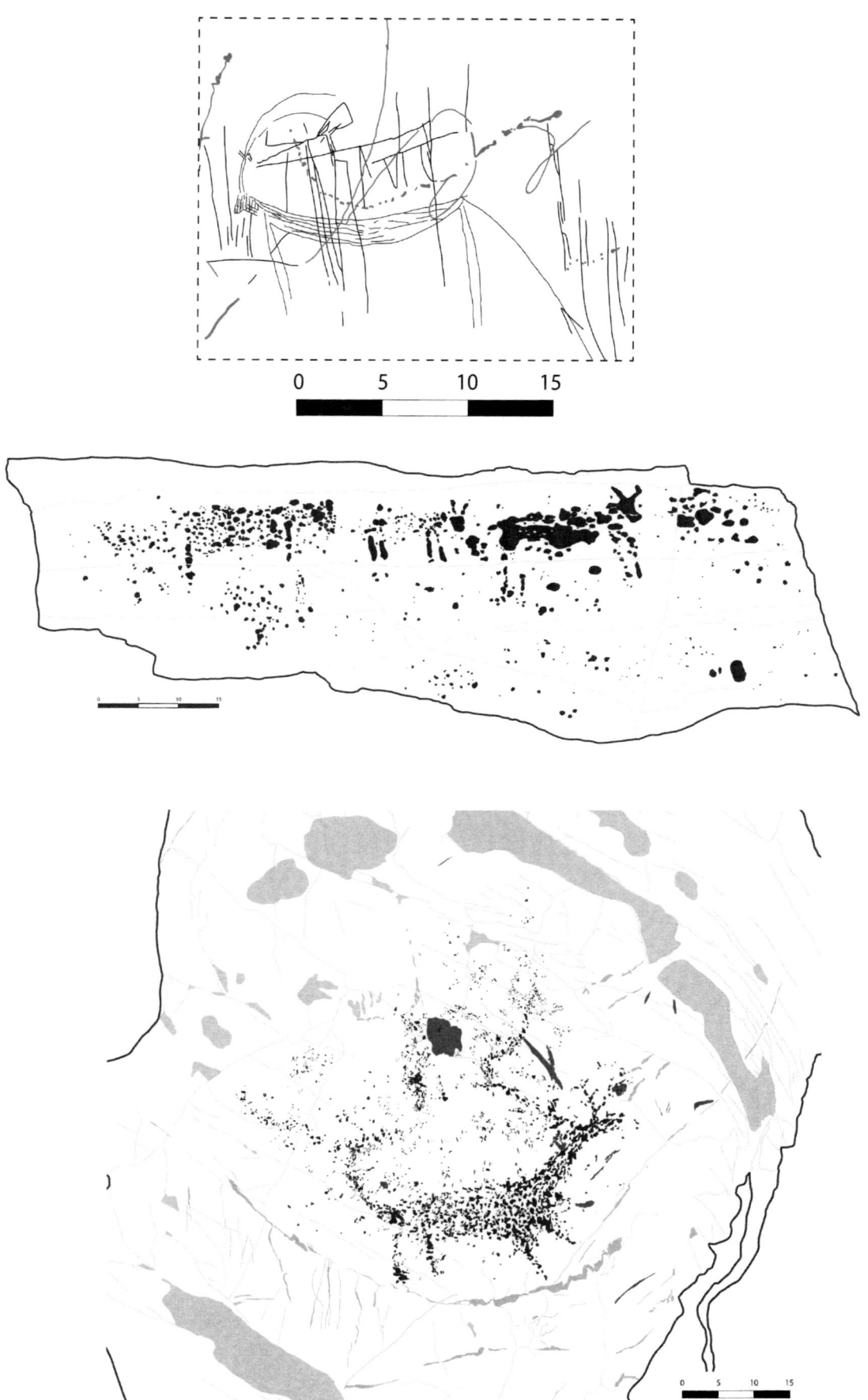

FIGURE 3. ROCK ART SITES OF RIBEIRA DA PEDRA DE ASMA 7, SANTO ANTÃO DA BARCA AND VEADO DO CABEÇO DO AGUILHÃO, IN SEQUENTIAL ORDER. ACCORDING TO FIGUEIREDO, XAVIER ET AL., IN PRESS.

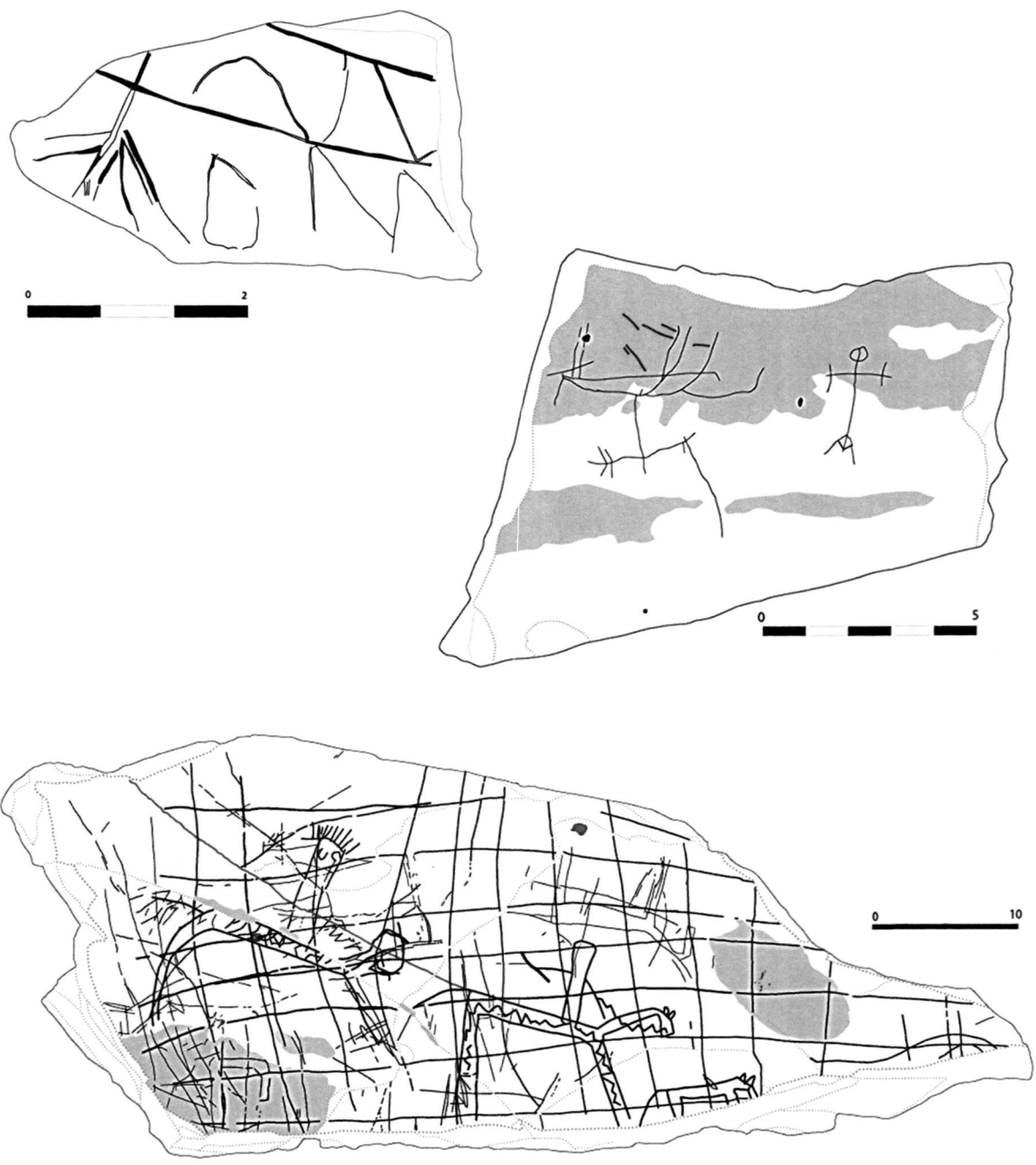

FIGURE 4. ENGRAVED PLAQUES FROM CRESTELOS WITH REPRESENTATIONS OF ABSTRACT AND GEOMETRIC MOTIFS, HUMAN DEPICTIONS AND RIDERS FIGURES. DRAWINGS BY FIGUEIREDO *ET AL*.

In the portable art collection of Crestelos, the raw material used was schist. Among the techniques used to engrave the slabs we were able to identify fine and superficial engraving, deep engraving, as well as picking. Concerning the figurative motifs represented, we were able to distinguish two main themes: horses and human figures. The depictions are rather schematic, done by the incision of simple lines that combine into simple forms. Nevertheless, in some plaques fine representations are found together with less carful depictions (Figure 4). In other cases, the small size of the figures is really impressive.

5. Through time, space, supports and figurative themes

As we already stated, our aim is to form an initial idea around the different contexts and supports of the figurative themes, found in a specific geographical area in the Sabor Valley, from the Palaeolithic till the Iron Age. With this in mind, the first issue we will address will be the organization of a space.

Taking into account the different supports on which rock art was found, mobile in the Palaeolithic and Iron Age, and fixed to the landscape in the recent Pre-History, our analysis will undoubtedly be reduced in chronological terms to the last mentioned period. When describing two of the rocks included in this chronological gap, Veado do Cabeço do Aguilhão and Santo Antão da Barca, we said that a real dynamic between these two rocks and the waters seem to have been created. In the first rock we have the representation of the male deer at winter, facing upstream to the female group, which in turn, is represented in the spring time when new-borns are to come. The female group is located precisely in the best pedestrian connection between both banks of the Sabor River; therefore, also being an optimal spot for the animals' water supply, and an area to fight for.

We believe that this shows a clear intention of the organization of space by recent Pre-Historic societies. It is also interesting to note that, unlike the Medal Terrace or the Crestelos area, which are both places of habitat (although in the first case the remains were somewhat decontextualized), the recent Pre-Historic places referred to in this text are only open air rock art sites, which were apparently not connected to any recognizable habitat site. This can be due to the disappearance of these sites or, to the fact that habitats were at the time situated at higher elevations, where no surveys were performed since they would not be affected by the hydroelectric project. The situation of funerary contexts and rock art sites located in the lower valley, as opposed to the location of habitat contexts at elevated levels, is also referred to in an area further down-stream in the Sabor River (Gaspar, May *et al.* 2014:34), which also denotes a certain organization of space.

It is quite interesting to note that the Palaeolithic is lacking evidence for open-air rock art and, in the Iron Age, the open-air rock art is not as visible as in recent Pre-History. Another interesting question is, why is portable art absent in recent Pre-History? This question may present us with some interesting ideas. First, until the discovery of Castelinho and Crestelos, portable art was rarely found in the Iron Age period, with few examples coming mostly from Portugal and Spain (e.g. Cosme, 2008; Meijide, Vilaseco and Blaszcyk, 2009). Also in the Palaeolithic, portable art is usually associated to the interior of caves, with some exceptions represented by Gonnersdorf (Germany) and Fariseu (Côa valley – Portugal). In recent Pre-History, besides the world of the *stelaes*, in this region there is no evidence for portable rock art. But very recently, an amazing piece was found in the Vilariça valley (close to the Sabor Valley), where recent Pre-Historic figures are represented on a schist slab. It is possible then that there is a world of recent Pre-Historic mobile art yet to be found, but its existence is associated with contexts that are found outside our studied geographic area. It is also important to stress that until the discovery of the first engraved plaque at the Castelinho Iron Age site, some engraved slabs were thrown away because no one was aware of the possibility of existence of these slabs. Ending our brief discussion about the supports of the engravings from different chronologies, it is curious to note that both in the Palaeolithic as in the Iron Age, the portable supports seem to be quite connected to the daily life of the communities.

We will finish this paper by presenting our thoughts on the figurative motifs. It should be stressed that we are only focusing on a specific geographical area, that once expanded could give us different results and, that the amount of data analysed in each period is not equal. But for now, and until full statistical analyses are realized, this is our state of the art.

In the following graphs of Figure 5, we can see the distribution of the different figurative themes in the Palaeolithic, recent Pre-History and the Iron Age. It is interesting to note that the widest range of

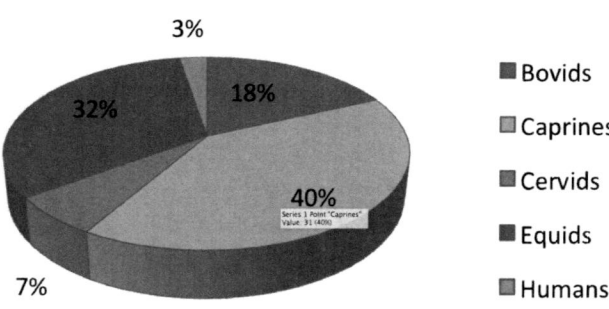

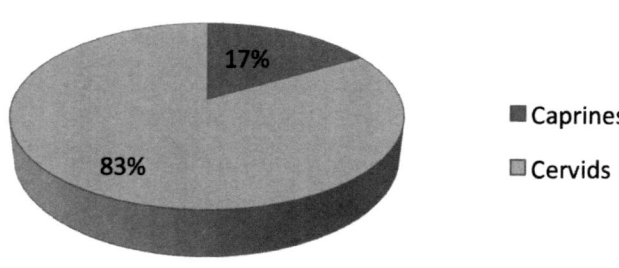

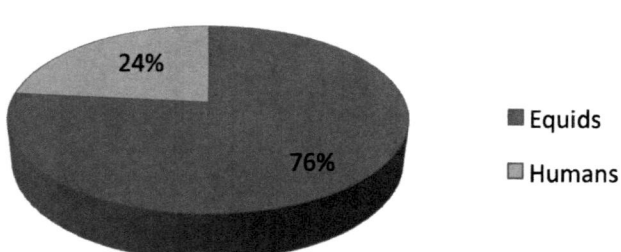

FIGURE 5. GRAPHS INDICATING THE PERCENTAGE OF FIGURATIVE MOTIFS REPRESENTED IN THE PALAEOLITHIC, IN THE RECENT PRE-HISTORY AND IN THE IRON AGE.

figurative representations is found in the Palaeolithic. Here we can observe the representation of aurochs, goats, deer, horses and humans. Contrary to what was expected, there are no anthropomorphic figures in the engravings from recent Pre-History, instead goats and mostly deer are the animals chosen to be represented. In the Iron Age the horses are the dominating theme, and are sometimes associated to human figures like riders.

In the Palaeolithic, the animals represented correspond to the same main four species represented in the Côa Valley Palaeolithic art: equides (horses), bovids (aurochsen), caprids (ibex and chamois) and cervids (red deer and *Cervus elaphus*). The distribution of the represented animals is closer to the one verified in the Cantabria, where Magdalenian style assemblages show a strong increase in the representation of goats, that is the dominant animal in El Bosque or Covarón (González Sainz, 2010: 40). Following this tendency, the rock from Ribeira da Pedra da Asma also exhibits a goat representation, although in a different style, that we can associate to Style V as proposed by Bueno, Balbín and Alcolea (2008). Already at a later period, somewhere in the recent Pre-History, the deer theme is resurrected, as we can see in the two rocks from Santo Antão da Barca and Cabeço do Aguilhão. In this period the deer seems to have a special meaning in all kinds of contexts. If we amplify the analysed area we can find its representations not only in carvings but also in paintings, both in open-air sites, such as Forno da Velha, as in megalithic tombs, such as Anta da Arquinha da Moura or Orca dos Juncais (e.g. Figueiredo and Baptista, 2010). During Iron Age, the themes suffer another turn and without any doubt the horses become the most represented figurative theme. We can state this unequivocally since the results we obtain in the analysis of the figurative motifs from Castelinho, where 521 slabs were studied, show consistent results. This demonstrates the importance of the horse, which when under human control, transformed transportation, warfare and trade among many other aspects of Iron Age populations (Bendrey, 2010: 10).

In summary, throughout Pre-Historic and Proto-Historic times, the depicted animals as well as their prominence is quite revealing. The wide variety of animals clearly demonstrate the importance or special meaning they had, both in an economic as well as in a spiritual sense. The disappearance of the representation of goats and horses in recent Pre-History must also be linked to the dramatic climate change and the predominance of some species over others.

6. Conclusions

This paper summarize results from a four-year field survey project that was undertaken as a result of the construction of a hydroelectric dam in the Northeast of Portugal. All the data collected is still under analysis and it will take some more years to get a clear picture of the meaning of the findings. Nevertheless, here we selected a small area, with a high concentration of rock art, to carry out a small case study regarding different temporalities, spaces, supports and ways of depicting figurative themes. On one hand our aim was to present some of the most important archaeological sites of the Sabor Valley to the scientific community through a summarized description. On the other, we wanted to stress some important issues that have been in our minds throughout this project. For instance, the importance of a whole new portable rock art collection that in this region seems to have reached two peaks: one in the Palaeolithic, the other in the Iron Age. As far as we know, there is no other place in Europe where portable art assumes such a huge importance, in such different human periods. So, could this be an isolated phenomenon or were other archaeological sites over-looked due to a lack of awareness of this kind of findings? Note that it is extremely difficult to recognize thin incised lines in schist surfaces during archaeological works. Another important issue addressed has to do with the long-term diachrony of the art manifestation at the Sabor Valley. We are perfectly aware that this is not an isolated case and we have to go no further than the Côa Valley to observe exactly the same reality. However, the lack of studies regarding the latest periods, the Iron Age and Historical periods, in our view, seems to limit a whole universe of information that could be extracted from rock art studies.

This article can be considered as a first and very preliminary attempt to overcome this situation. Although we have only discussed figurative themes, and we have gone no further than the Iron Age, the numerous occurrences of rock art at the Foz do Medal terrace, Ribeira da Pedra de Asma, Santo Antão da Barca, Cabeço do Aguilhão and Crestelos, makes a much broader investigation desirable and probably possible in a near future.

Bibliography

BAPTISTA, A. M. 2009. O Paradigma Perdido: O Vale do Côa e a Arte Paleolítica de Ar Livre em Portugal. Edições Afrontamento. Parque Arqueológico do Vale do Côa.

BENDREY, R. 2010. The Horse. In O'Connor, T.; Sykes, N., eds. – Extinctions and Invasions: A Social History of British Fauna. Windgather Press. p. 10-16.

BUENO RAMIREZ, P.; BALBÍN BEHRMAN, R.; ALCOLEA GONZÁLEZ, J. 2008. Estilo V el ámbito del Duero: Cazadores finiglaciares en Siega Verde (Salamanca). In R. de Balbín Behrman, R. ed. – Arte Prehistórico al aire libre en el Sur de Europa: actas. Junta de Castilla y León. Consejería de Cultura e Turismo. p. 259-286.

COSME, S. R. 2008. Proto-história e Romanização entre o Côa e o Águeda. In III Congresso de Arqueologia, Trás-os-Montes, Alto Douro e Beira Interior: Proto-história e Romanização – Guerreiros e Colonizadores. 3, p. 72-80.

FIGUEIREDO, S. S. 2013. A Arte Esquemática do Nordeste Transmontano: Contextos e Linguagens. PhD Thesis, Minho University, Braga, Portugal.

FIGUEIREDO, S. S.; BAPTISTA, A. M. 2010. As pinturas esquemático – simbólicas do Forno da Velha (Lagoa, Macedo de Cavaleiros): um diálogo entre a arqueologia e a geologia. In Bettencourt, A.; Alves, L. B. eds. – Dos Montes, das pedras e das águas: Formas de interacção com o espaço natural da pré-história à actualidade. CITCEM. APEQ. p. 11-24.

FIGUEIREDO, S. S.; NOBRE, L.; GASPAR, R.; CARRONDO, J.; CRISTO ROPERO, A.; FERREIRA, J.; SILVA, M. J. D.; MOLINA, F. J. 2014. Foz do Medal Terrace- An Open Air Settlement with Paleolithic Portable Art. INORA. 68, p. 12-19.

FIGUEIREDO, S. S.; NOBRE, L.; CRISTO ROPERO, A.; XAVIER, P.; GASPAR, R.; CARRONDO, J. (in press) – Reassembly Methodology in Paleolithic Engraved Plaques from Foz do Medal Terrace (Trás-os-Montes, Portugal). Sobre rocas y huesos: las sociedades pré-históricas y sus manifestaciones plásticas. Conference Proceedings of the III International Meeting of Doctorates and Post doctorates: Art in Prehistoric Societies. p. 432-443.

FIGUEIREDO, S. S.; XAVIER, P.; SILVA, A.; NEVES, D.; DOMÍNGUEZ GARCÍA, I. (in press) – The Holocene Transition and Post-Palaeolithic Rock Art from the Sabor Valley. Sobre rocas y huesos: las sociedades pré-históricas y sus manifestaciones plásticas. Conference Proceedings of the III International Meeting of Doctorates and Post doctorates: Art in Prehistoric Societies. p. 192-203.

GASPAR, R.; MAY, A.; DONOSO, G.; TERESO, J. 2014. O Abrigo Natural do Lombo das Relvas, um local de enterramento no Neolitico final/Calcolítico inicial?. Al-madan. II série. n. 19 (Tomo I), p. 25-35.

GONZÁLEZ SAINZ, C. 2010. Unidad y Variedad de la Región Cantábrica y de sus Manifestaciones Artísticas Paleolíticas. Las Cuevas con Arte Paleolítico en Cantábria. ACDPS. p. 29-45.

MEIJIDE CAMESELLE, G.; VILASECO VÁZQUEZ, X. I.; BLASZCZYK, J. 2009. Lousas decoradas com círculos, cabalos e peixes do Castro de Formigueiros (Samos, Lugo). Gallaecia. 28, p. 113-130.

SANTOS, F.; SASTRE, J.; FIGUEIREDO, S. S.; ROCHA, F.; PINHEIRO, E.; DIAS, R. 2012. El sitio fortificado del Castelinho (Felgar, Torre de Moncorvo, Portugal). Estudio preliminar de su diacronía y las plaquetas de piedra con grabados de la Edad del Hierro. Complutum. 23:1, p. 165-179.

SASTRE, J. 2014. Da Idade do Ferro à Romanização da área de Crestelos. Actas do I Encontro de Arqueologia do Mogadouro. Mogadouro. p. 79-94.

Archaeological field survey in the *Erqueyez* site (Western Sahara): new discoveries of rock art

Teresa MUÑIZ LÓPEZ
Research Group Lemgasem. C/ Calderón de la Barca, 5, 2º izq, 18006 Granada,
tmuizlpez@yahoo.com

Ahmed KHATRI
Museum Tifariti (Western Sahara)

David GARCÍA GONZÁLEZ
Research Group Lemgasem

Carmina LÓPEZ-RODRÍGUEZ
Andalusian Institute of Earth Sciences (CSIC-UGR)

Abstract

Here we present preliminary results from an archaeological survey carried out in the Erqueyez Lemgasem *archaelogical site, massif located in the Western Sahara. During the field survey numerous* taffonis *with rock art were located in the area as well as described in previous studies. The study was supported by a cooperation project between Saharawi and Spanish researchers.*

Key words: *Western Sahara, field survey,* taffoni, *rock art*

Résumé

Dans ce travail nous présentons les résultats préliminaires de la campagne de prospections archéologiques réalisée dans le site de Erqueyez Lemgasem, au Sahara Occidental. Cette dernière a permis d'augmenter le nombre de cavités ornées de peintures rupestres. Divulguées dans diverses publications jusqu'à nos jours. Le travail de recherche a été effectué dans le cadre d'un projet de coopération entre chercheurs espagnols et sahraouis.

Mots-clés: *Sahara Occidental, prospection,* taffoni, *peintures rupestres*

1. Introduction

We present the results of an archeological survey campaign that was implemented in the archeological site of Erqueyez (Western Sahara). This survey was developed in the framework of a research and cooperation project.

Apart from finding new *taffonis* with rock art, the experience carried out has made a breakthrough in the formation of a group of local archaeologists in order to achieve the objective of carrying out research projects in a position of equality with respect to the numerous researchers of international teams that work in the area of the Western Sahara.

As a result of previous exploration work carried out by different research teams it is possible to find published articles and monographs about numerous taffonis with rock art (Pastor y Carrión, 1996, p. 47-48; Soler *et al.* 1999; Muñiz, 2005, p. 6-11; Soler, 2007, p. 107-420). However, dimensions and geological features of this massif favor the existence of a large number of taffonis and small cavities that are likely to harbor paintings, conditioning in this way the existence of many areas still without prospect, especially in the western slope of the rocky massif.

In this way, the objective of the archaeological intervention carried out by Saharawi and Spanish archaeologists was to intensively explore areas that had not previously been prospected and to increase the knowledge about the graphic demonstrations of the massif of Erqueyez.

2. Geographical and geological synthesis

If we look at the previous works that have been developed within this study area (region of Zemmour) we observe that the names used to refer to the zone vary sometimes. The most recurrent terms are Rekeiz Lemgasem (Soler, 2007, p. 107) or Erqueyez (Muñiz, 2005, p. 1), both based on transcripts of the local language.

The limits of this region are not well defined. It is located in the north east of the Western Sahara, and it also occupies part of Mauritania. Its northern boundary is located in the region of the Saguia El Hamra and its southern limit would be located to the east of the city of Dakhla, formed by several topographic elevations such as the Um Dreiga, Kab Ennaga and Negyir along the plains and valleys of Bir Nazaran.

In general, the climatology of the area coincides with that of the Western Sahara, being characterized by the short duration of the wet season and the presence of torrential rains. If you look at the scenery that surrounds the Erqueyez massif, it is possible to recognize natural watercourses or "uadis" formed by episodes of heavy rainfall as well as the generation of deep canyons, as a product of the sporadic rains.

The area of the Zemmour is characterized by the presence of small elevations, such as the one that shapes the Erqueyez massif, which stands out among the vast plains that surround the place (Fig. 1). The massif describes an elongated shape from south west to north east, with a height that ranges from approximately 600 m and 400 m at its southwestern and northeasterns extrems, respectively. Its

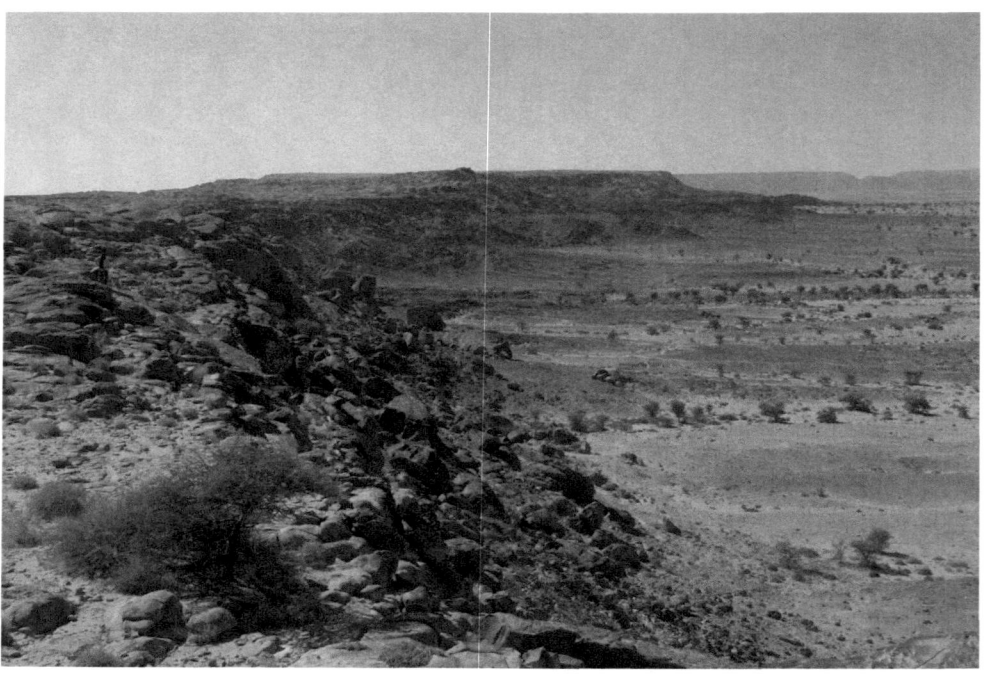

FIGURE 1. VIEW OF THE WEST SIDE OF THE MASSIF OF ERQUEYEZ LEMGASEM.

longitudinal axis is about 14 km, being much more narrow the transverse axis, with distances ranging between 0.5 and 1 km (Fig. 1).

The landscape that surrounds the massif of Erqueyez does not present the classic image of the sandy desert formed by dunes, but an extensive flatness, known as stony desert or hamada. The existence of underground water and low rainfall maintain the local vegetation composed of shrubs and grasses. Part of this vegetation is the Talha, a tree of the family of Acaciae that is characterized by its large spines.

The knowledge of the geology of the area is crucial, due to the existence of several geological formations which host panels with graphic demonstrations.

The Western Sahara territory is located in the west African platform. This platform is composed of rocks that were formed more than 2000 Million year ago. Those rocks were eroded long before the Precambrian period and represent pieces of a primitive continental crust.

This platform is covered by sedimentary deposits formed during intermittent events of accumulation and rising, being afterwards folded and eroded as a result of active tectonic processes (Guiraud et al. 2005, p. 92). At the end of the Precambrian period, the orogeny that causes the formation of the Mountain Chain of the Antiatlas promotedan intense process of metamorphism and a series of tectonic movements resulting in the fracturing of the oldest basement and the appearance of rock cracks and the generation of magmatic processes (Hefferan et al. 2000, p. 91).

The stratigraphic sequence of the massif of Erqueyez is constituted by a lower unit composed of granite rocks and dated as Precambrian in age (>600 M.y.). Above this interval, a sedimentary interval is reported, mainly composed of quartzarenitebeing dated as Ordovicic in age (440-590 M.y.). This upper stratum is thought to have been formed under relatively shallow marine conditions, affected by metamorphism processes after their emplacement.

During the Late Paleozoic, these materials were folded and exposed to processes of erosion and weathering as a result of climatic variations at that time. Such erosional processes promoted the generation of cavities, the increase of fissures as consequence of rock dissolutions, or the detachment of blocks, favouring the occurrence of protected areas where extensive repertoire of panels with graphic demonstrations are located, and that nowadays form the whole rock art of Erqueyez.

These cavities in the rock hosting the paintings are called taffonis. Their origin is due to processes of physical and/or chemical weathering of the rocks. In the massif of Erqueyez, the wind shock may constitute an important factor to take into account for the taffonis generation. This, the wind would contribute significatively, throughout the transport of numerous grains of quartz that may impact on the rocky surface eroding the substrate.

Simultaneously, the extreme thermal amplitude reported in the area may induce the fracturing of rocks, since during the day they supports very high temperatures and expand themselves, while by night the temperature drops and the rock collapses, producing the onion skin weathering effect.

3. New discoveries of rock art in the West area

During the prospecting work there were located about thirty unpublished rock shelters with cave paintings. The majority of them were found in the west face of the massif, which is the least prospected area, as has been highlighted in the introduction to this document.

In our research we have selected eight rock shelters, because they have the best preserved paintings. The variables that caused a better conservation of these paintings are related to the fact that they are located in places more shielded from the erosive agents (Fig. 2).

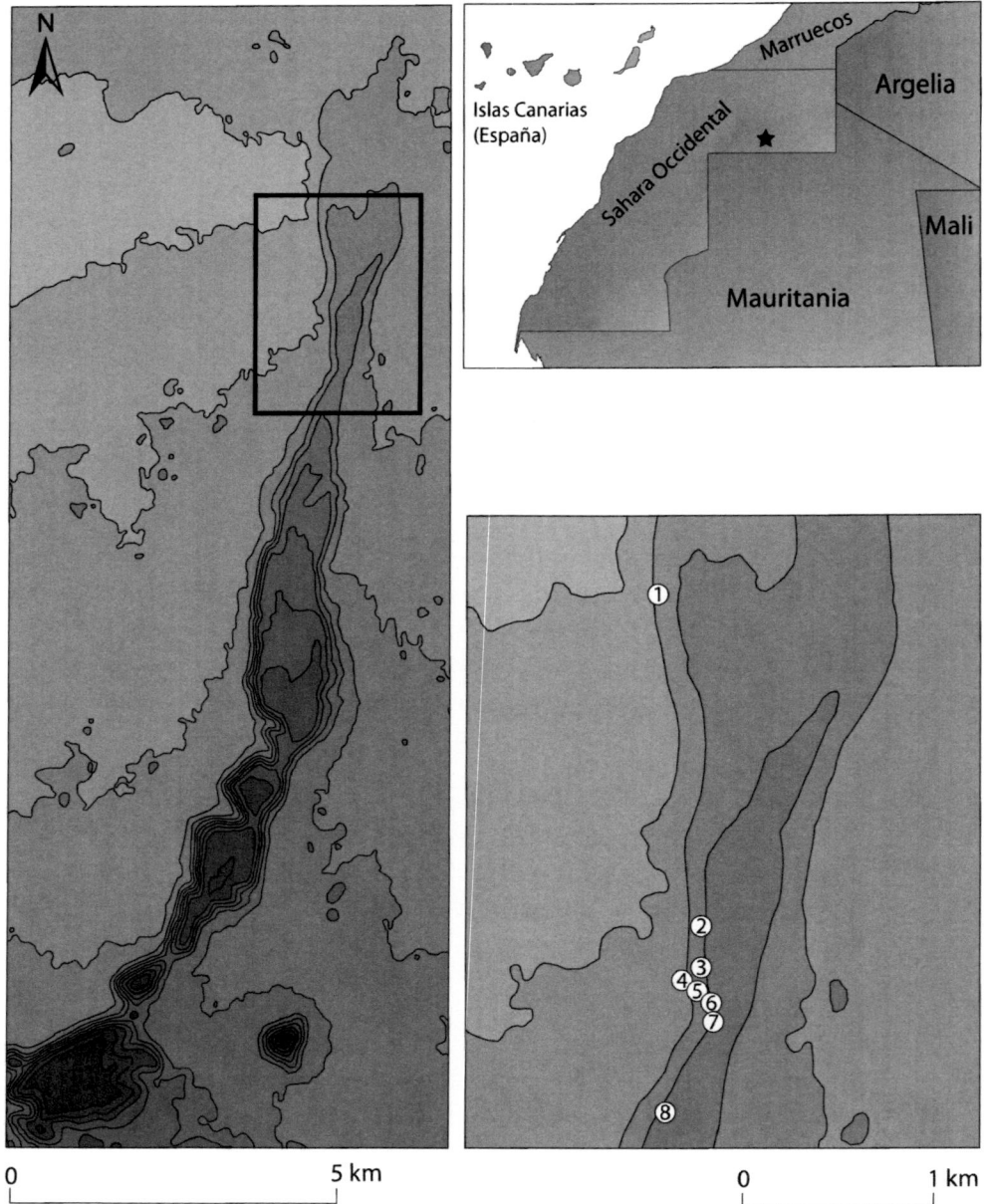

FIGURE 2. MAP SHOWING THE LOCATION OF THE SHELTERS DESCRIBED IN THIS PAPER.

3.1 Description of the rock art

The criteria that we used for the description of the paintings are aspects related to its location in the rock shelter, their morphology, color, and conservation status.

Shelter 1

This rock shelter is prominent because it has a large number of motives represented, having been able to count up to fourteen figures that stand out for their good state of conservation in comparison with the rest of the cavities chosen in this work. The paintings are located in the central area of the panel constituting a scene where there are some indefinite strokes, animals and human figures.

The human figures presents some specific features very little present in the whole graphic demonstrations in *Erqueyez*. Those are very stylized figures and even excessively elongated, comparable with the *tazina* style (Soler, 2007, p. 634; Fraguas, 2009, p. 98) (Fig. 3 and 4A) that appear in an attitude of running, by going to the right side of the panel. Along with these very well plotted figures where you can observe the garnet stroke and the fill, there is another painting conducted in a very schematic manner and lighter in color.

With regard to the animal figures they vary in their size and composition, but they are still figures of large dimensions (20 x 10 cm approx.), and possibly gazelles, arranged in row. They are blurring as they move toward the right of the panel (Fig. 4 C and D). The first of these animal figures is located next to the human figures, and it is a silhouette that only preserves part of the body, hind legs and neck. Isolated from this group of gazelles there is a garnet painting of an animal that could be identified as a bird (Fig. 4 B).

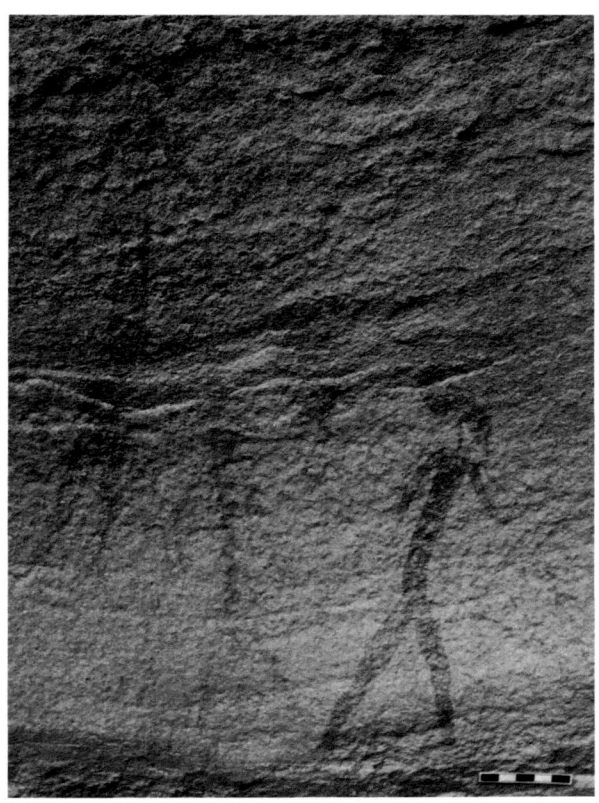

FIGURE 3. DETAIL OF GRAPHIC MANIFESTATIONS OF HUMAN FIGURES IN SHELTER 1.

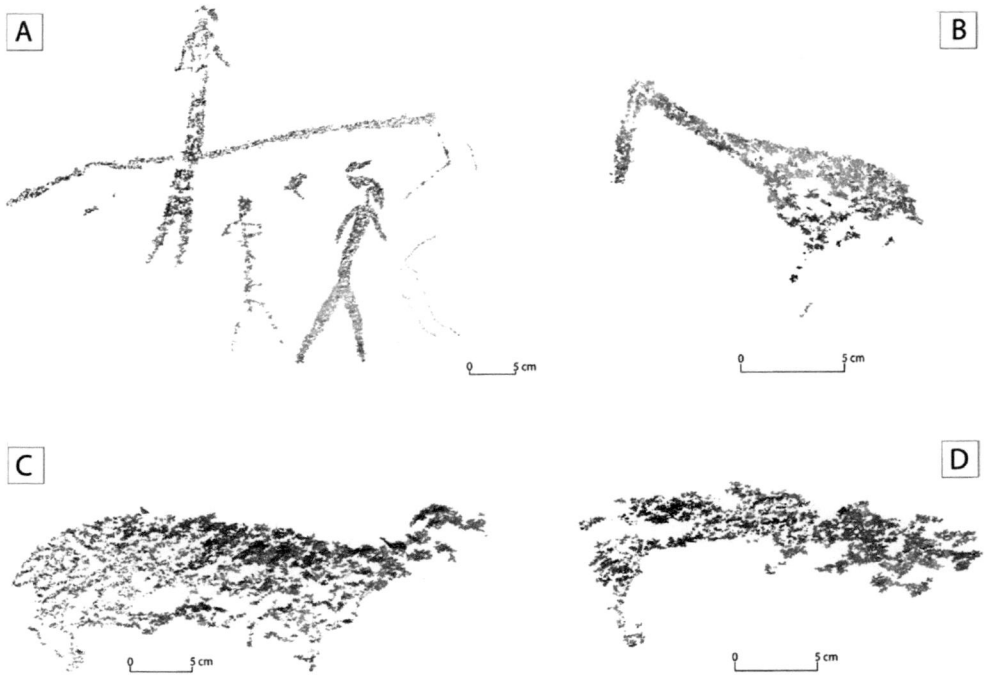

FIGURE 4. CALQUE OF THE REPRESENTATIONS THAT ARE DOCUMENTED IN SHELTER 1.

The rest of the paintings of this small cave are indeterminate lines in a poor state of conservation. It stand out a long line that presents a stroke slightly arched, of approximately one centimetre thick and lighter in color to the rest of the figures. This line overlaps one of the human figures described above (Fig. 4 A).

In summary, in addition to exceptional paintings in *Erqueyez,* this complex panel offers different forms of representation and colors, which might indicate that we are faced with graphical demonstrations carried out in different historical moments.

Shelter 2

Despite its surface (5 x 3 m approximately), we only found the representation of two human figures, one as opposed to the other and in an attitude of movement, without being able to specify the action that is taking place. Both are located in the middle area of the shelter and are made in dark red color using a fine contour and fillied of the same tone in a uniform manner (Figs. 5 and 6).

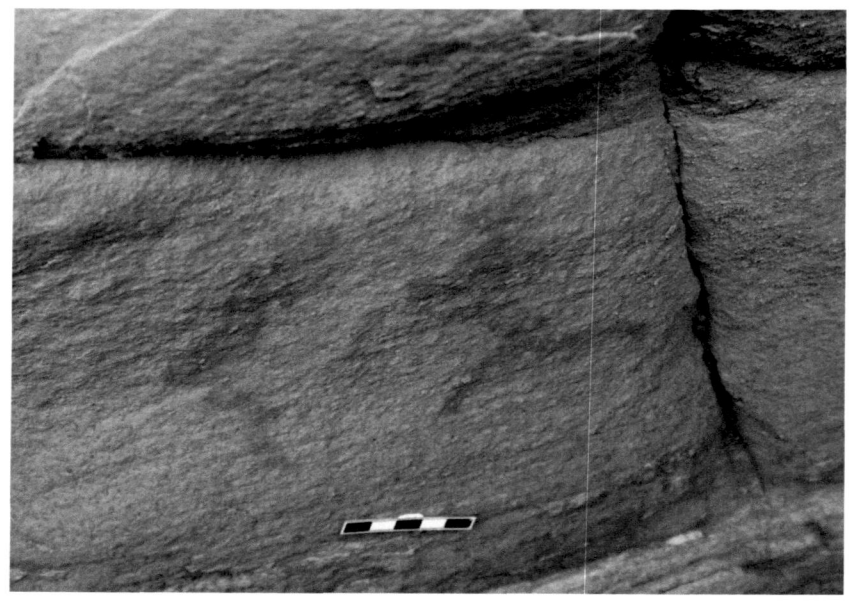

FIGURE 5. DETAIL OF GRAPHIC MANIFESTATIONS OF HUMAN FIGURES IN SHELTER 2.

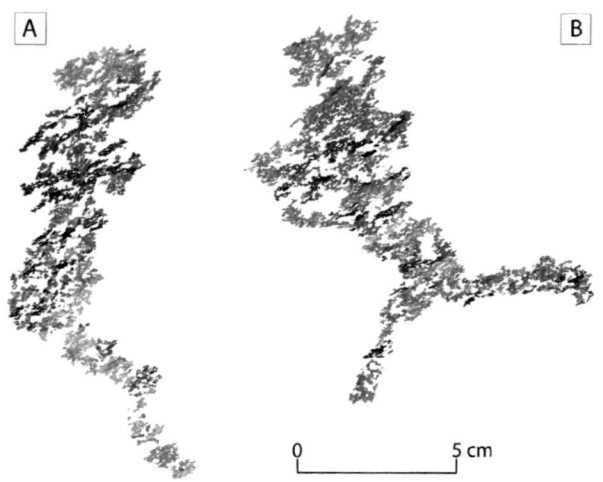

FIGURE 6. CALQUE OF THE REPRESENTATIONS THAT ARE DOCUMENTED IN THE SHELTER 2.

Shelter 3

Looking at the location of this shelter, it is located in the upper platform that forms the Erqueyez massif and it is oriented to the south, while the rest of previously described cavities in this work are in the west and in the rocky outcrop. The two figures in red represented in this *taffoni* have a very poor conservation status, as it is not currently possible to determine the reason and if they are animal or human figures (Fig. 7).

Shelter 4

All the motives are located in an area of difficult access and the paintings are in a shelter with a very small space between the floor and ceiling (approximately 0.5 m). There are two representations of ostriches very well plotted, one above the other, in dark maroon color.

In spite of the fact that the paintings are sheltered from erosive agents, they present simultaneously blurred areas and other areas in very good condition. Morphologically they are much similar to the figures of ostrich documented in other shelters that are described later, presenting in this case a better state of preservation (Figs. 8 and 9).

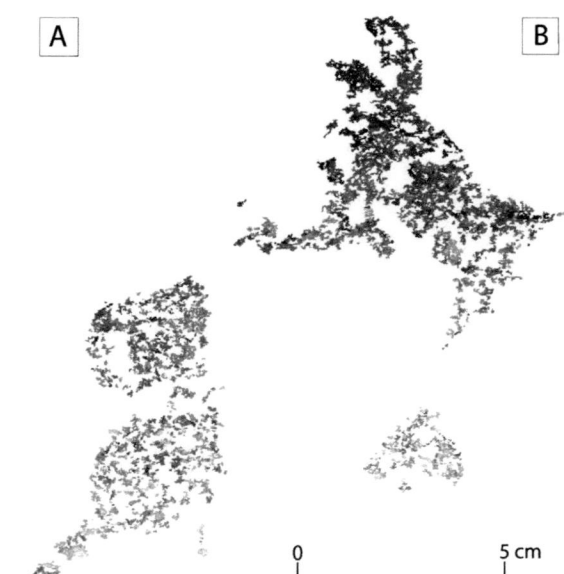

FIGURE 7. CALQUE OF THE REPRESENTATIONS THAT ARE DOCUMENTED IN THE SHELTER 3.

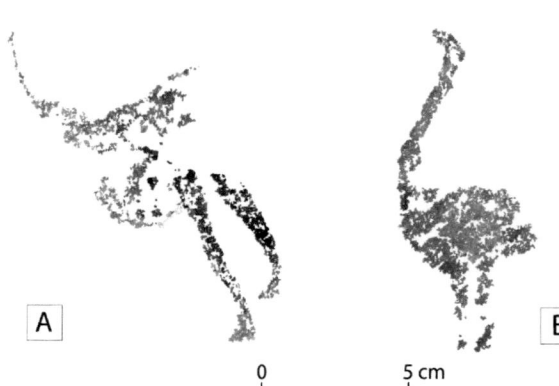

FIGURE 9. CALQUE OF THE REPRESENTATIONS THAT ARE DOCUMENTED IN THE SHELTER 4.

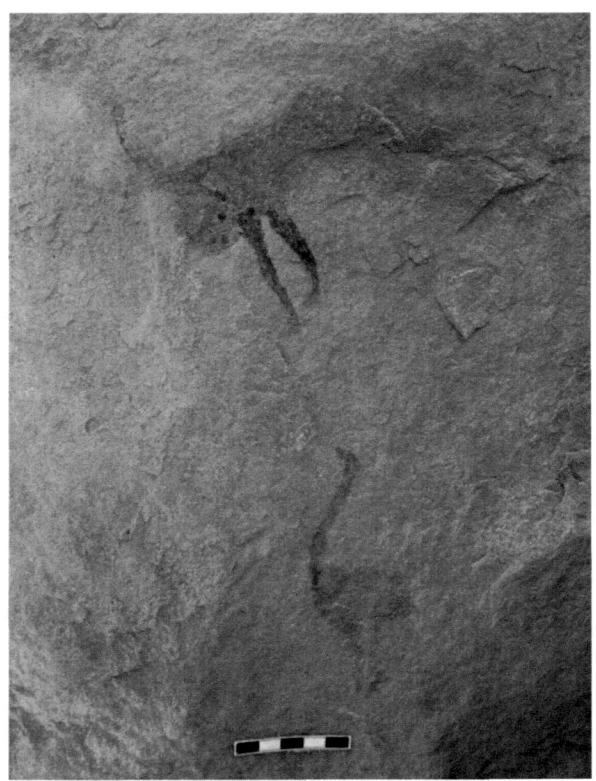

FIGURE 8. DETAILS OF GRAPHIC MANIFESTATIONS OF ANIMALS FIGURES IN SHELTER 4.

Shelter 5

In this cave it highlights the peculiar morphology of its *taffoni*, formed by the action of wind erosion on a large block detached from the ledge and transported by gravity to its location. We found five

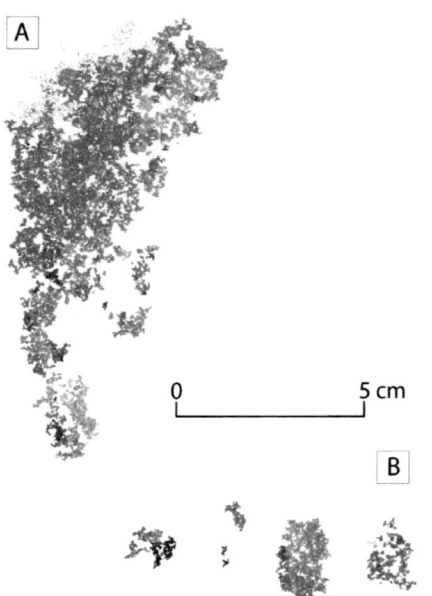

FIGURE 10. CALQUE OF THE REPRESENTATIONS THAT ARE DOCUMENTED IN THE SHELTER 5.

maroon motives, one of greater size (approximately 10 cm) and the other four in fingering form. The paintings are affected by erosive agents as flaking of the panel, solar radiation or wind action, which makes identification of the figures depicted (Fig. 10).

Shelter 6

The *taffoni* presents a number of motives that show different degrees of conservation, while some so corrupted that it has not been able to make the digital tracing or establish the motive represented. With regard to the motives that were analyzed in more detail, there are several animal figures, five in total, identified as ostriches. All of them are incomplete preserved, and only the lower extremities are still visible in three of them (Fig. 11 C, D and E) and neck and head in the remaining (Fig. 11 A and B).

Shelter 7

The morphology of the shelter determines that some of their motives are located in an area of difficult access. To collect information about them we had to lie down on the floor of the *taffoni*, as the paintings were located on the roof in a space delimited by a height less than a meter. Those paintings were protected of erosive agents, such as solar radiation and wind action providing its good conservation status.

The representation group is formed by two animal figures (Fig. 13 B and C) and a human in a departure attitude (Fig. 13 A). It is remarkable that this human figure is carrying an object behind his back. The animal figures have very stylish extremities and a great level of detail in the representation of elements such as the tail (Fig. 12 and 13).

Superimposed on one of these animal figures there is the silhouette of an animal figure painted in black with a very fine line and higher dimensions than the rest of the motives (Fig. 13 D). Both the overlay as the technique for preparing this figure reveals a more recent chronology. By now we cannot determine the time elapsed between the developments of the two figures.

The characteristics of this figure seem to lead to the conclusion that it is a representation

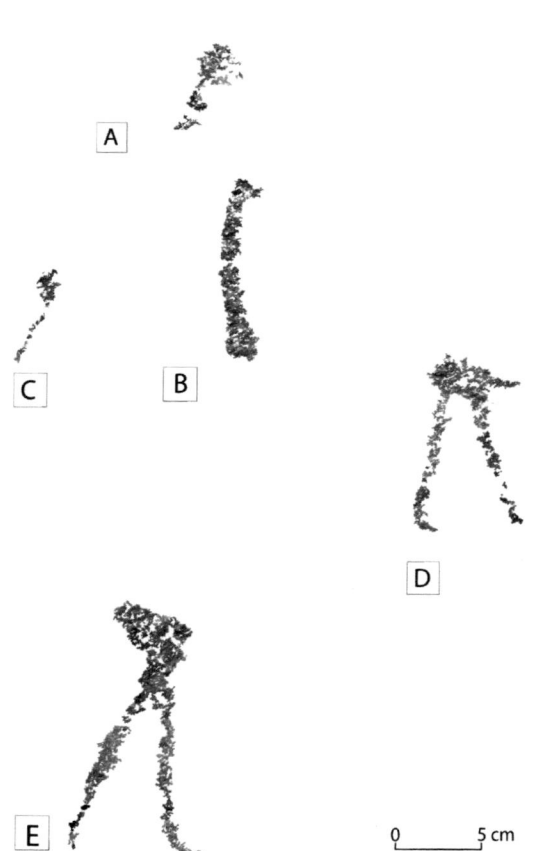

FIGURE 11. CALQUE OF THE REPRESENTATIONS THAT ARE DOCUMENTED IN THE SHELTER 6.

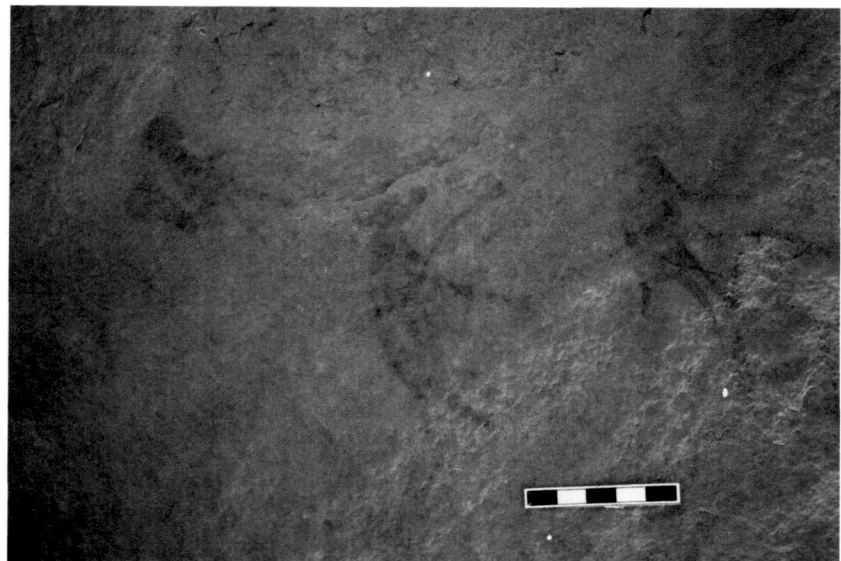

FIGURE 12. DETAIL OF GRAPHIC DEMONSTRATIONS IN THE SHELTER 7.

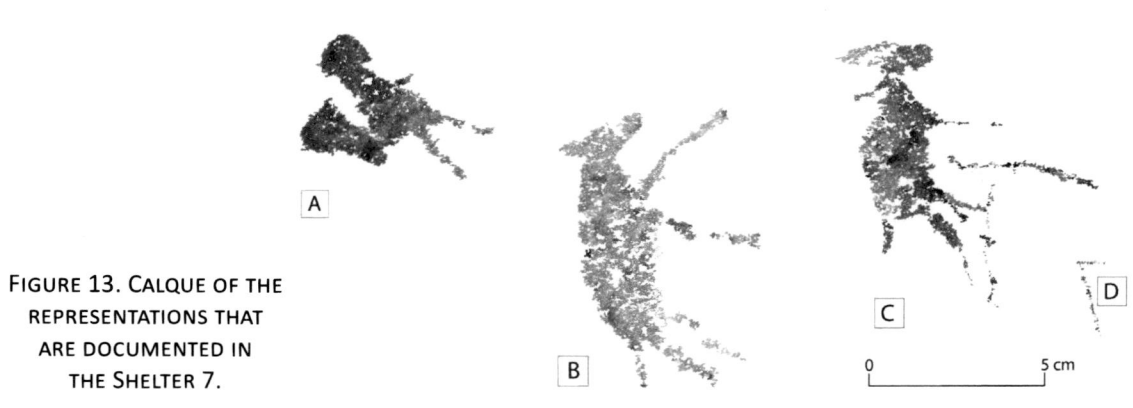

FIGURE 13. CALQUE OF THE REPRESENTATIONS THAT ARE DOCUMENTED IN THE SHELTER 7.

of a gazelle. The head, neck and the top of the spine have been drawn with a thin line, obviating the extremities and the lower part of the body. Next to this figure and below of the described above we document a representation in red, whose shape and state of conservation does not allow us to identify the motive represented. Due to the small space between the ground and the panel, located on the roof, we have not been able to obtain a suitable photographic documentation of these last two motives described nor the panel in its entirety.

Finally, in a more external *taffoni* area, we found a series of fine lines, similar to those documented in the first shelter described in this document, and a fingering figure in dark maroon color.

Shelter 8

This is a shelter of small dimensions, approximately two meters of panel, where we have documented two typologies of manifestations; one consisting of fine linear strokes and the other with two motives whose conservation status does not allow us to infer the represented figure (Fig. 14). It should be noted that being on the inside of the shelter, we have an ideal point of observation of the flatland that surrounds the *Erqueyez* massif, which is framed by the morphology of this *taffoni* (Fig. 15).

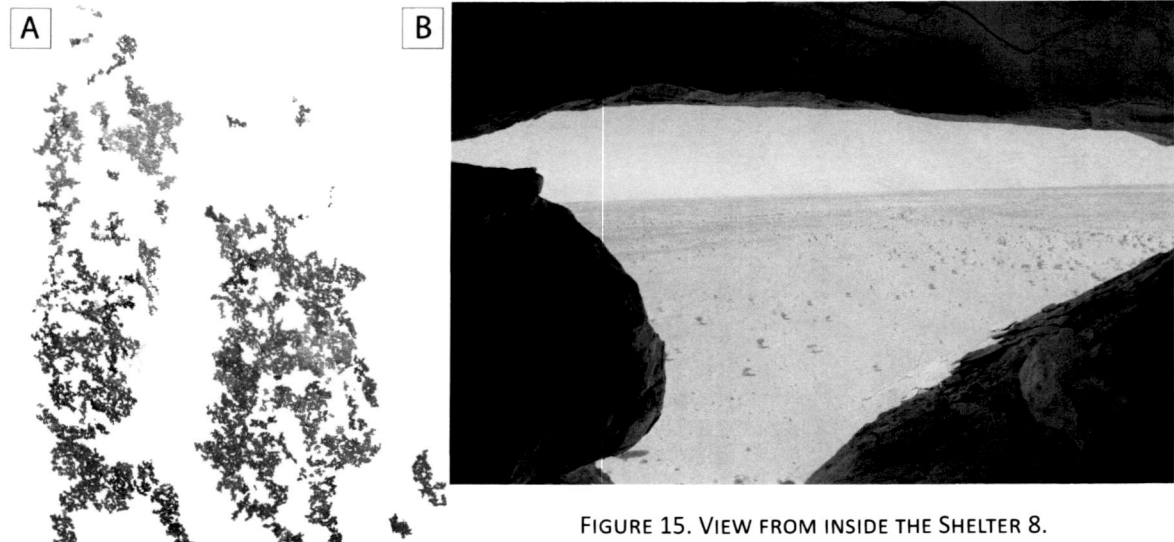

FIGURE 15. VIEW FROM INSIDE THE SHELTER 8.

FIGURE 14. CALQUE OF THE REPRESENTATIONS THAT ARE DOCUMENTED IN THE SHELTER 8.

4. Conclusions and prospects

Prospecting in the framework of the *Cooperation Project for Local Staff Training to offer Guide Services and Interpretation of the Archaeological Site of Erqueyez (Western Sahara)*, have made possible to us to document new rock shelters, within the limits of this archeological complex, and connecting to those who had already been released in previous publications.

In the motives described in this work, we can find human figures, animals, delicate strokes and representations unable to identify by now. Another typology present in the manifestations of the *Erqueyez* graphic that has not been documented on this occasion in any panel, is the impression of hands in positive (Muñiz, 2005, p. 9).

In relation to the colors that were used the predominant is the red color, except for the animal figure made with a fine black line described in the shelter 7. If we look at the set of graphic demonstrations of *Erqueyez*, we can observe that the red color is the one that presents the highest proportion, even so we also find motives that combine this with white color and to a lesser extent in black colour.

In connection with the graphical demonstrations identified as human figures, there are attitude of movement for various actions, in some of them complemented with hauling of some objects, such as is the case of the shelter 7, and the carrying of headdress, as in the shelter 1.

The human figures accompanied by an object are frequently found not only in the set of graphic demonstrations documented throughout the massif of *Erqueyez*, but in many stations of rock art. In their research works in the Levantine Iberian Peninsula various researchers have been interpreted elements with similar characteristics as an archer quiver for the transport of arrows (Blasco, 1974, p. 50; Domingo, 2005, p. 168). Even so, we cannot rule out the possibility that it could be another type of objects, such as baskets for the transport, agricultural work and harvest or something to carry childs.

In regard to headdress, it seems to be related to the representation of symbolic actions such as dances or elements of personal adornment, and whose ethnographic parallels in the two cases are very numerous, as is the case of the Karo of Ethiopia or the Surma and Mursi that inhabit in the Omo Valley, on the border of Ethiopia and Sudan.

Linked to the motives of animal figures, the identification of the represented taxa constitutes a tool of great interest in paleoenvironmental reconstruction of the territory at the time of production of the graphics demonstrations. Studies carried out in the past on a broader sample of motives in the massif of *Erqueyez*, have revealed that a big number of the animals represented are giraffes (*Giraffa camelopardalis*) and gazelles (*Gazella spp*). Other animals that appear in the shelters are cattle (*Bos taurus*), ostriches (*Struthio camelus*), elephants (*Loxodonta africana*), rhinoceros and some taxa identified as belonging to the group of antelopes (*Tragelaphus strepsiceros*, among others) and carnivores (*Canidae* and *Felidae, Hyenidae*) (Pleguezuelos and Sanchez, 2003, p. 164-165). In the case of the small caves described in this work, the animals were composed mainly by caprinae, gazelles or ostriches.

One variable that have been demonstrated to be on a recurring basis throughout this work- and also expressed in various summaries made by other researchers in the area- is the problem of a chronological allocation of the graphics documented in the area of study. Up to now we do not have an absolute dating of the paintings. Proposals for a chronological order have been carried out based on the study of the fauna represented or comparing styles and shapes with other figures of North Africa (Soler, 2006, p. 21; Soler *et al.* 2006, p. 137). In this way it has been determined that the pictorial activity have had its start about 3800 BP and persisting until a change of era. Most of the representations of the area would belong to the Zemmur prehistoric period (Soler, 2007, p. 648-650).

In addition, up to date there have been no documented in an accurate way any places of habitat of susceptible populations that could make the graphical demonstrations. We have only identified some areas related to the manufacture of utensils or lithic objects of adornment. In our survey we document and describe graphical symbols and we were able to observe remnants of lithic industry on the floor of some of the *taffonis*, that means a carving activity. We documented laminar nuclei, as well as some sheets along the remains of carving and technological process as strikers. Associated with these materials we also observed the presence of ceramic fragments and remnants of ostrich egg shell. These egg shells are related to beads made in this material and we found finished products and elements in manufacturing stage.

As a whole and in response to the characteristics of the materials documented, they would be associated with epipaleolithics and neolithic contexts.

However, in the case of observations on surface material and taking into account the fact that the territory has a series of exceptional qualities that motivated a long occupation of this space by various populations over time, we have to take into account several premises when we want to associate these industries to the graphical demonstrations.

For that reason it is necessary to emphasize on the study of the areas of lithic production or adornment objects through the realization of archaeological explorations. This is to determine the possible chrono-cultural relationship of these shelters with graphic demonstrations and move forward in the knowledge of the societies that lived there.

The prospecting activity described in this work highlights the need to continue in the line of recognition of the terrain, since new graphic demonstrations have been documented in areas that had been previously prospected. This is related to the complex orography that presents the massif of *Erqueyez* but also with other factors which must be taken into account, such as the incidence of light on the small caves at different hours of the day that could cause good or bad visibility conditions for paintings. At the same time, although we focused our research in remote areas, the extension of the massif causes that there are still areas that have not been prospected with intensity.

Aknowledgments

We want to express our gratitude for their invaluable help for the realization of this work to the following individuals and entities: ARTifariti, Museum of Tifariti, Mohammed Baecha Salama, Luchaa Saleh, Matala Saleh Chej, Abdel Fatah, León González Pérez, Nursery Service of the Archaeological Complex of *Erqueyez*, personnel of the Polisario Front, Ruth Muñiz López, Sarah Bachs and Lamin Seraoui.

Bibliography

BLASCO BOSQUED, Mª. C. 1974. La caza en el arte rupestre del Levante español. Cuadernos de prehistoria y arqueología, Nº 1, Universidad Autónoma de Madrid, p. 29-55.

DOMINGO SANZ, I. 2005. Técnica y ejecución de la figura en el arte rupestre levantino. Hacia una definición actualizada del concepto de estilo: Validez y limitaciones. Universitat de València. p. 471. Tesis Doctoral.

FRAGUAS BRAVO, A. 2007. Del panel a la hegemonía: Nuevas teorías y tecnologías para el arte rupestre del Noreste de África. Universidad Complutense de Madrid. p. 591. Tesis Doctoral.

GUIRAUD, R.; BOSWORTH, W.; THIERRY, J.; DELPLANQUE, A. 2005. Phanerozoic geological evolution of Northern and Central Africa: An overview. Journal of African Earth Sciences 43, p. 83-143.

KEVIN, P.; HEFFERAN, H.; KARSON, J. A.; SAQUAQUE, A. 2000. Anti-Atlas (Morocco) role in Neoproterozoic Western Gondwana reconstruction. Precambrian Research 103, p. 89-96.

MUÑIZ LÓPEZ, T. 2005. Los abrigos con pinturas rupestres de Erqueyez (Tifariti, Sahara Occidental). Prospección arqueológica: diseño y resultados. Arqueología y Territorio, 2, Universidad de Granada, p. 1-17. Available at URL: http://www.ugr.es/~arqueologyterritorio/Artics2/Arti2_1.htm

PASTOR MUÑOZ, M. y CARRIÓN MÉNDEZ, F. 1996. Los primitivos pobladores del Sáhara Occidental. El yacimiento arqueológico de Erqueyez, Tifariti. En Las ciudades perdidas de Mauritania: expedición a la cuna de los Almorávides. Fundación El legado andalusí. Granada, p. 43-52.

PLEGUEZUELOS GÓMEZ, J. M. y SÁNCHEZ PIÑERO, F. 2003. Fauna actual y representada en los abrigos de Erqueyez: Implicaciones paleoecológicas. En El complejo arqueológico de Erqueyez (R.A.S.D.). Sáhara Occidental. Memoria de Investigación. CICODE & Universidad de Granada. p. 164-165.

SOLER SUBILS, J. 2006. Peintures préhistoriques tardives du Zemmour (Sahara Occidental). International Newsletter on Rock Art, 45, p. 15-23.

SOLER SUBILS, J. 2007. Les pintures rupestres prehistòriques del Zemmur (Sahara Occidental). Documenta Universitaria. Col·lecció Tesis, Girona, 690 p. Tesis Doctoral.

SOLER, N.; SERRA, C.; ESCOLA, J.; UNGÉ, J. 1999. Sáhara Occidental. Passat i present d'un poble. Sáhara Occidental. Pasado y presente de un pueblo. Universitat de Girona, Fundació privada Girona. Universitat i Futur. Girona, 216 p.

SOLER, J.; SOLER, N.; SERRA, C. 2006. The painted rock-shelters of the Zemmur (Western Sahara), Sahara. Prehistory and History of the Sahara, 17, 129-142.

Measuring the spatially-related perceptibility of prehistoric rock art. Some initial notes

Carlos RODRÍGUEZ-RELLÁN
Fernand Braudel-IFER Scholar. Fondation Maison des Sciences de l'Homme.
Pôle scientifique, 190 avenue de France, 75648, Paris, France
GEPN, Dpto. Historia I, Facultade de Xeografía e Historia, USC,
Praza da Universidade, 1. 15782, Santiago de Compostela, Spain

Ramón FÁBREGAS VALCARCE
GEPN, Dpto. Historia I, Facultade de Xeografía e Historia, USC,
Praza da Universidade, 1. 15782, Santiago de Compostela, Spain

Abstract

Galician open-air rock art has been often considered as an active element in the configuration of the economic and symbolic signification of prehistoric landscapes. Thus, in the last 20 years, the spatial setting of petroglyphs was analysed and repeatedly linked to the control of certain resource-rich areas or the routes leading into them. Nevertheless, such considerations have frequently sidestepped the importance of the decorated panels perceptibility as a key factor in determining their agency over the landscape. The use of GIS and high-resolution cartography will allow us to make an initial appraisal of such aspect.

Keywords: *visibility, perceptibility, rock art, petroglyphs, viewshed*

Resumen

El arte rupestre al aire libre de Galicia ha sido frecuentemente considerado como un elemento activo en la configuración de la significación económica y simbólica del paisaje prehistórico. A lo largo de los últimos 20 años, la distribución espacial de los petroglifos ha sido analizada y repetidamente asociada con el control de determinadas areas ricas en recursos o con las rutas que llevan a las mismas. Sin embargo, tales consideraciones han ignorado con frecuencia la importancia de la perceptibilidad de los paneles decorados como un elemento fundamental en la determinación de su agencia sobre el paisaje. Mediante SIG y cartografía de alta resolución abordaremos el análisis espacial de este aspecto.

Palabras clave: *visibilidad, perceptibilidad, arte rupestre, petroglifos, cuenca visual*

1. Introduction

The Galician territory, in the Northwest of the Iberian Peninsula, is characterized by the presence of a vast Post-Palaeolithic rock art phenomenon, comprising c. 3400 open-air rock art sites (Vázquez *et al.* this volume). The most comprehensive study of the catalogue conducted so far evidences how most Galician petroglyphs (approx. 84%) display geometric images –mainly cup-marks and an assorted array of circular motifs– while there is also a numerically minor naturalistic group, made up fundamentally of animal (deer and horses) and weaponry representations (daggers and halberds). Both groups show also distinct geographical distributions: the geometric motifs are more widespread, reaching well into inland Galicia, while the other is concentrated in the coastal areas, only the weapons occurring occasionally in more interior locations (Ibid.).

To establish a chronological framework for North-western Iberian rock art is not an easy task. The shallow and heavily eroded soils in the immediate surroundings of petroglyphs make very difficult the preservation of archaeological remains that would have made possible to date the engraving episodes. Overcoming such setbacks has been done by matching certain engraved motifs to known parallels in the archaeological record, the comparison with similar examples from other areas or the scant archaeological information recovered in the vicinities of some petroglyphs (Fábregas and Rodríguez-Rellán 2015). These methods have made possible to date, with reasonable certainty, the main carving activity of Galician petroglyphs in the 3rd and 2nd millennium BC, although some motifs might have roots in the local Neolithic and, likewise, certain carved surfaces retained a degree of significance even into historical times.

Given its special richness, the Galician rock art phenomenon has been studied over the past 150 years. Such an endeavour has not been carried out only by local specialists, since reputed foreign archaeologists such as H. Obermaier, E. MacWhite, E. Anati or R. Bradley paid attention to this topic. As reported in other European regions (Goldhahn *et al.* 2013), most traditional approaches to the study of Northwest Iberian petroglyphs were characterized by the consideration of rock art sites as little more than 'artistic objects', analysed in isolation from their place in the landscape and the society that had produced them.

However, this situation was challenged in the 80s and 90s. Mainly due to local circumstances – the strength of the 'Landscape Archaeology', the economic and institutional barriers to conduct archaeological excavations or the impact of specific studies (e.g. Bradley 1997)– specialists began to explore the spatial distribution of rock art and their relationship with other prehistoric remains. Thenceforward, dozens of studies have followed that approach to Galician rock art (Rodríguez *et al.* 2008; Santos and Criado 2000; Villoch 1995).

The influence of authors such as Ingold (1987) or Casimir (1992), led to many of these studies interpreting the open-air rock art of areas such as Galicia as an intermediary and normative element of the land tenure among farmer groups who –while still very mobile– exploited the same resources but who were unlikely to meet on a regular basis (Bradley 1997). In this context, rock art would act as a kind of 'intergroup' communication mechanism –a sort of code of signals or messages– designed to mediate in the use of the landscape, establishing preferential or exclusive access to specific spaces with an economic and/or symbolic significance. Thus, petroglyphs would be linked to the so-called 'geography of movement', their location analysed in terms of proximity to key transit points, such as cols or mountain ridges, and also to small basins providing shelter, water and pasture along the year (Bradley 1997; Bradley *et al.* 1994; Criado 1999).

2. Perceptibility of rock art

The interaction between petroglyphs and landscape is basically mediated through three parameters: location, visibility and perceptibility. **Visibility** refers to the amount of space seen from a specific petroglyph, and it depends almost exclusively on the place where this is located. Visibility can be restricted to a close area surrounding the petroglyph or, otherwise, exerted to medium or even long distances. This divergence could point to a different role of the petroglyphs: the first disposition might imply a potential close-range 'control' of the space; in the latter, it is exerted from afar, so the interaction would be less obvious and, maybe, more symbolic (Fábregas and Rodríguez-Rellán 2015).

The analysis of petroglyphs' viewshed, either through direct observation or GIS tools, has played a major role in establishing the aforementioned link between rock art and specific areas of the landscape, such as allegedly major pathways or spaces that were symbolically and economically important for the prehistoric communities (Bradley *et al.* 1994). Furthermore, the existence of visual relationships with other archaeological sites was used as a resource to assign the chronology of a specific petroglyph (Fábregas 2010; García and Santos 2004).

Meanwhile, the analysis of **perceptibility** –or a petroglyph 'ability' of being perceived or noticed from the surroundings– has been systematically neglected by most specialists, who have automatically considered rock art as a phenomenon whose contemplation would have been little restricted, just because it was outdoors. Moreover, perceptibility has often been confused with visibility and, when considered, its analysis was limited to the size and inclination of the engraved panel, identifying the petroglyphs displayed on vertical surfaces as those more perceptible (Peña and Rey 2001).

However, other characteristics must be considered also when analysing the potential perceptibility of rock art: leaving aside the –presently unproven– possibility of the carvings being also painted, there are other ways to fine-tuning the perceptibility of the engravings, taking advantage, for instance, of the sharp contrast in colour between freshly made grooves (lighter) and the untouched granite (usually dark grey). Eventual refreshing of the engravings would keep that contrast for some time. On the contrary, the selection of light-toned granite rocks would difficult the contemplation of the carvings, their perception depending a lot from the incidence of the sun light at certain times of the day (or the year, sometimes). Other conditions may be at play too: the rain can change slightly the colour and brightness of the granitic outcrops and also the wet surfaces, when catching the light, 'raise up' the carved images. (Fábregas and Rodríguez 2015). Besides, vegetation may have also served as a method to hide many of the petroglyphs, making them virtually invisible even from the immediate vicinity (Brown *et al.* 2011), evidencing that remoteness might have not been the only way of seclusion for open-air rock art.

Furthermore, it is also commonly accepted that the understanding of meanings of rock art would have largely depended on the domain of culturally mediated processes. Therefore, symbolic or mental restrictions for the watching of rock art might have been almost as effective as physical constraints. Not only it would be important the command of the symbols and scenes displayed, but also the control of the 'mise-en-scène': a set of physical, mental and emotional activities including the approach to the rock, standing by it or the sequence in which the motifs and scenes should be watched (Tilley 2008) and even the precise knowledge of the proper conditions as to weather and illumination.

While the culturally driven aspects acting in the perception processes of rock art remain virtually unapproachable for non-informed studies, some of the other, more 'tangible' aspects, are susceptible of analysis. That is the case of the spatially related perceptibility of rock art: the potential perceptibility of rock art deriving from its location in the landscape. Although relatively easy to analyse, especially thanks to the modern GIS tools, such aspect was seldom taken into account by the specialists.

3. Material and methods

In this paper, the potential spatially-related perceptibility of rock art sites of Northern Barbanza (A Coruña) is analysed. The Barbanza (Figure 1) is the northernmost of the peninsulas that make up the Rías Baixas and can be divided into two extensive topographical units of great biogeographical diversity. On one hand, there is the Sierra, a thinly populated mountain range with an average height of about 550 m. It serves as the watershed between the Arousa and Muros-Noia Rias. On the other hand, there is a long coastline with both sandy beaches and rocky cliffs, behind which lies a rather narrow coastal plain.

After intensive survey of the study area, we have compiled a catalogue of 164 carved rocks in the council of Porto do Son, closely corresponding with the Northern section of the Barbanza. The systematic collection of data about the sites within our study area has revealed some patterns in the location of the carved rocks. We observed that most petroglyphs (62%) are found at heights of between 100 and 300 m, although the land within that range amounts to just 34% of the study area. Thus, the engravings are concentrated in what we can consider as a buffer zone between the two main geographical features of this region: the sierra and the coastal platform. On a more detailed level, the carvings are mostly on slopes (34%) with an unusually good command of the coastal plain, and less commonly in what may have been transit areas such as terminal ridges (22%) or mountain passes (4%). Of course, several sites depart from the norm: a few are found at the coastal

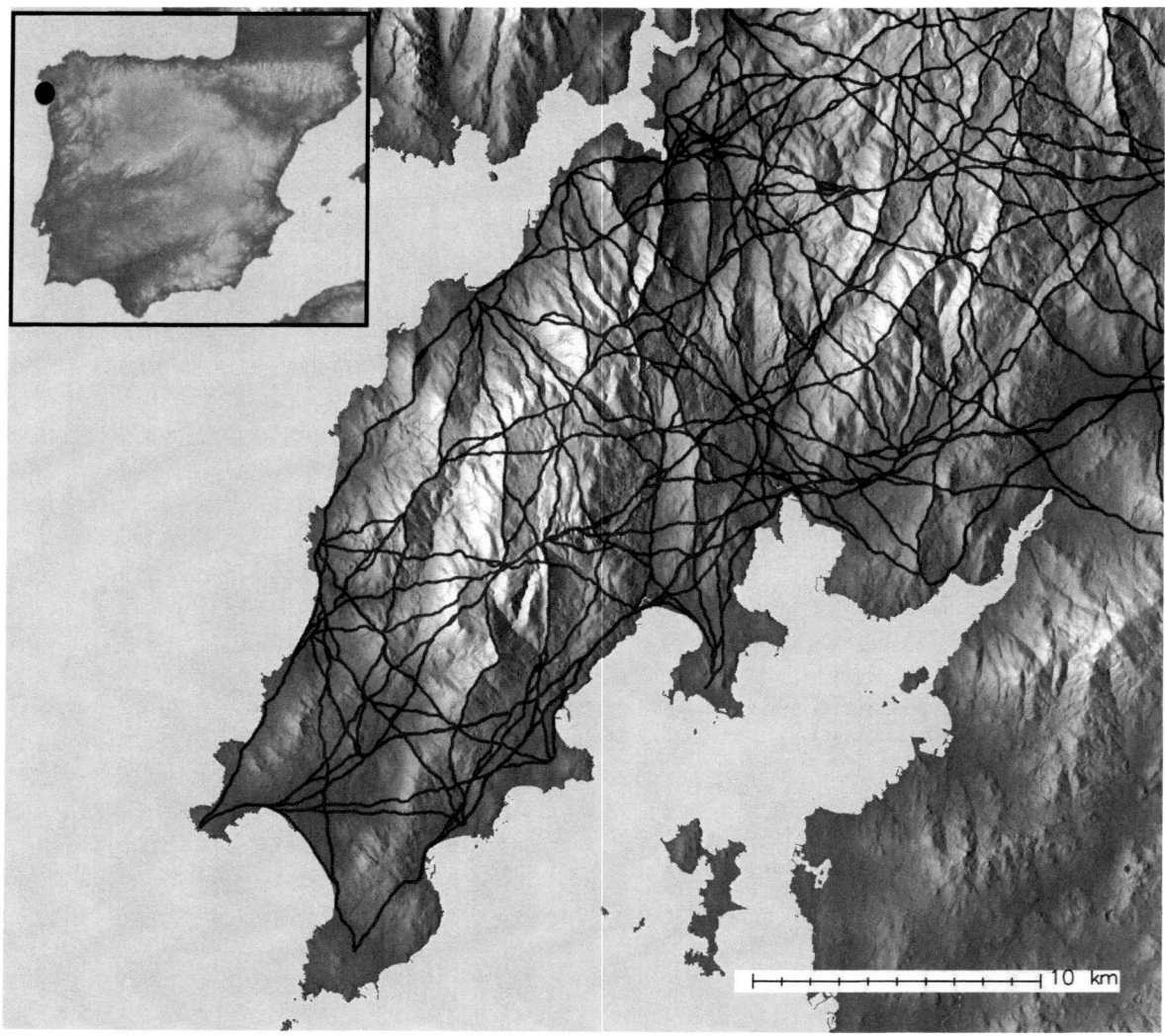

FIGURE 1. LEAST-COST PATH NETWORK LINKING DIFFERENT POINTS OF
THE BARBANZA PENINSULA (A CORUÑA).

plain, while others occur at higher altitudes or even on top of the sierra (Fábregas and Rodríguez 2012a).

The study area stands out for the numerous representations of animals (generally deer), together with the other classical motifs of Atlantic rock art, such as cup marks and circular motifs. Weapons, hunting/riding scenes or human figures are seldom found. There are also a number of historic carvings such as crosses.

One of the most striking aspects of this study relies on the fact that most petroglyphs in the study area were done on horizontal, flat exposures (57% of the cases against 7% on vertical), so that they disappear from view only a few metres away from the rock. This suggests that, as a rule, the engravings were not meant to be viewed from a distance. Such impression was subsequently supported by the discovery of petroglyphs within rock shelters not only in the study area, but also in other Galician regions (Fábregas and Rodríguez 2012a). Furthermore, the analysis conducted during the fieldwork suggested that more than half of the petroglyphs are not located near 'major pathways' and, even then, the visual relationship is not always obvious: in many cases, petroglyphs are barely perceptible from the latter. Thus, the evidences derived from our survey pointed out that open-air rock art in the study area would have not been as openly accessible and closely related to transit areas as traditionally suggested.

In order to corroborate this hypothesis, we have conducted a simple spatial analysis of the study area using GRASS GIS 6.4 and 7.0 (http://grass.osgeo.org) and a 5 meters resolution Digital Elevation Model (DEM) derived from the Plan Nacional de Ortofotografía Aérea (PNOA), carried out by the Instituto Geográfico Nacional of Spain. Using these tools, we have calculated a net composed by 250 least cost paths linking different areas of the Barbanza Peninsula (Figure 1). For this, we have first created several maps of anisotropic cumulative cost of moving along the landscape in which both altitude, slope and presence of watercourses has been taken into account. Least cost paths were subsequently calculated using the GRASS utility *r.drain* (http://grass.osgeo.org/grass64/manuals/r.drain.html), which allowed us to obtain a somewhat reallistic estimate of those areas trough which walking would have been less costly in terms of energy consumption.

The choice of the beginning and endpoints for the calculation of the transit routes was made independently of the location of the rock art sites to be studied, thus avoiding an overrepresentation of the spatial relationship between sites and transit routes which has been detected in previous studies on the study area (Villoch 1995). Instead, were calculated the least cost paths between those areas thought to be the more likely habitation areas of the prehistoric populations responsible for the engraving of petroglyphs: the coastal platform and the inner valleys of the Barbanza Peninsula (Fábregas and Rodríguez 2012b).

The calculation of such a dense network of least cost pathways allowed us the identification of those areas with a higher probability of being transited and that, therefore, could be considered as 'statistically defined key points' in the transit along the study area. If the notion of petroglyphs as linked to the 'geography of movement' holds true, at least a significant percentage of rock art sites should be located close to these pathways.

However, it must be noted that –in areas with a rugged microrelief– spatial proximity does not necessarily implies close relationship. For example, a rock art site located only 20 meters away from a major pathway might be impossible to be noticed from it, due to –for example– the presence of small ridges or outcrops. In order to try to detect this kind of issues we have implemented a GIS-based analysis focused on detecting how the location in the landscape of a given petroglyph might affect its potential perceptibility from the major pathways through the landscape.

We find somewhat contradictory that –although traditionally linked to the 'geography of movement'– the analysis of the relationship between petroglyphs and transit has almost always been centered in the motionless element of this equation: the rock art. Thus, it is the visual command (i.e. visibility) held *by* petroglyphs *over* pathways and other areas what has been used as a basis for evidencing the role of the former in the shaping of the prehistoric landscape (Bradley *et al.* 1994; Santos and Criado 1998). However, it might be argued that at least part of the intended audience of petroglyphs would have been located not in the sourroundings or on top of the carved surfaces, but walking through such pathways. Therefore, in order to correctly assessing the agency of rock art over the surrounding landscape its potential for being noticed (i.e. perceptibility) must also be taken into account in our analysis.

To that purpose, we have conducted an 'inverse viewshed' analysis that was carried out not from the petroglyphs but from the least cost paths previously defined (Figure 2). For this, we have automatically generated points every 300 meters along these routes. As a result, more than 7000 points have been created. Subsequently, a viewshed analysis has been carried out from each one of these points. Given the high number of analysis to be made, this process was carried out by using I. Ullah's *r.viewshed.cva.py* (http://grass.osgeo.org/grass64/manuals/addons/r.viewshed.cva.py.html),

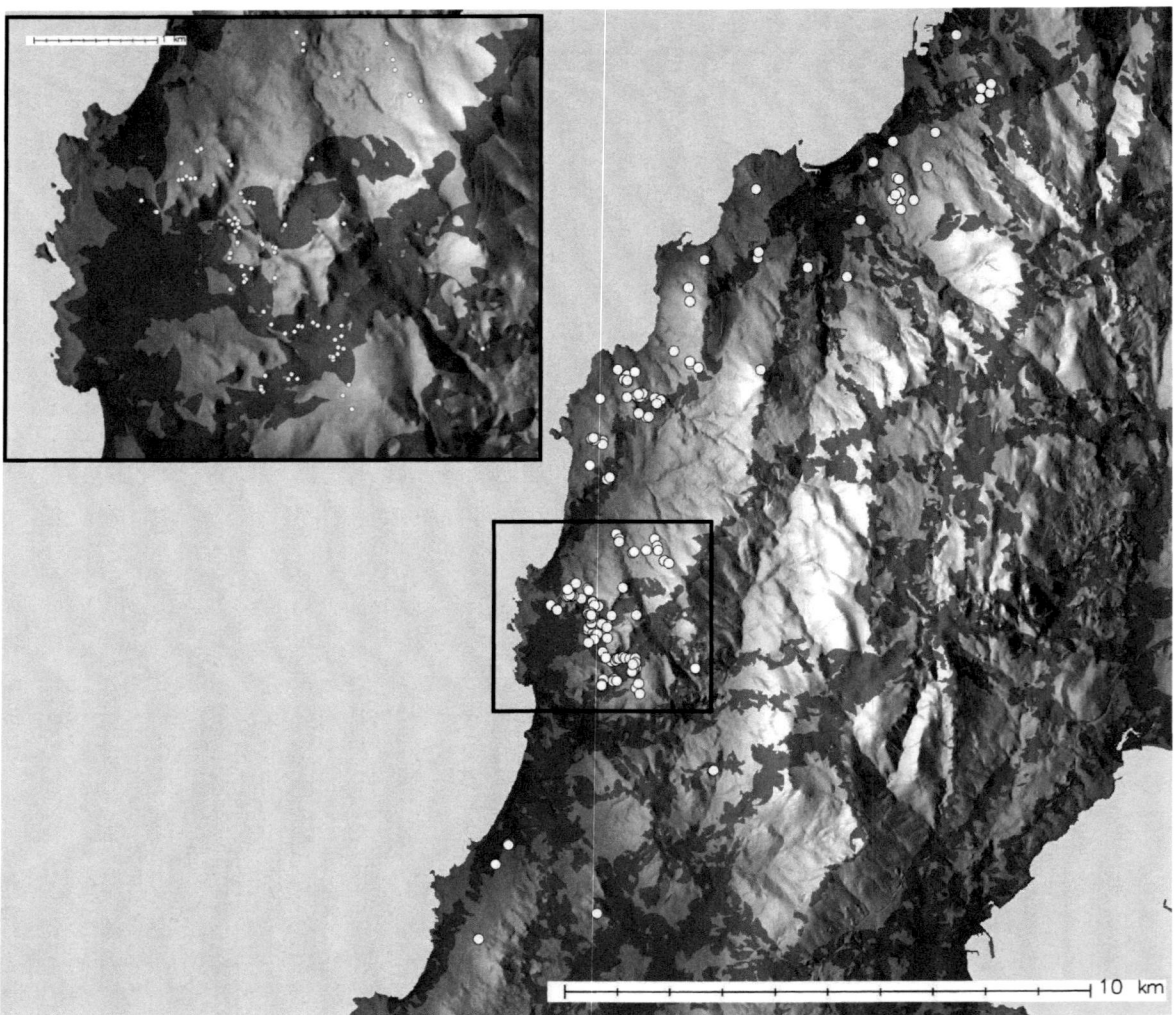

FIGURE 2. 'INVERSE VIEWSHED' OR CUMULATIVE VIEWSHED (DARKER TONES)
CARRIED OUT FROM THE LEAST COST PATHS. WHITE POINTS:
ROCK ART SITES LOCATED IN THE PORTO DO SON COUNCIL.

a module for GRASS that allows the calculation of 'cumulative viewshed' or 'visualscape' maps from a series of input points. The approximate duration of this analysis was 25 hours.

The maximum distance for calculating this cumulative viewshed was established in 300 meters. This yardstick was chosen because it was the maximum distance at which the vast majority of rock art sites (both the rocks and the motifs) remain perceptible from the sourroundings, although most sites were barely visible at distances of only 50 meters. The latter distance is equivalent to that mentioned for the British and Scandinavian petroglyphs in which such circumstance has been noted by specialists (Bradley 2002; Ling 2006). Thus, the results achieved by our analysis should be considered as an optimistic estimate of the perception of North Barbanza petroglyphs from major pathways.

4. Results

The measuring of the distance between petroglyphs and major pathways is 278 metres on average, with no significant differences between rocks displaying different types of motifs (Kruskal-Wallis chi-squared = 0.5554, df = 5, p-value = 0.99). Of the 164 rock art sites, 65 (39.6%) are beyond 300 meters of any major pathway, while 29 (17.6%) are separated for 500 meters or more.

In the light of these results readers may assume the existence of a close relationship between rock art sites and paths in the study area. However and as we have stressed in the former section, such an assumption must be handled with care when dealing with rough terrains as those in the study area, where relief can isolate or separate areas in *Euclidean* proximity to each other. As a matter of fact, the analysis of the 300 meters 'inverse viewshed' conducted from the major pathways evidences how 97 of the 164 petroglyphs (59.1%) are not perceptible from those. Again, no significant differences between motifs (Kruskal-Wallis chi-squared = 0, df = 5, p-value = 1) can be detected although some groups of motifs, such as zoomorphs and prehistoric varia (weapons, ride scenes, etc.), tend to be located in areas that make them slightly more noticeable (Figure 3), somehow supporting the impression advanced in previous works (Bradley 1997; Peña and Rey 2001).

The comparison between the spatial-related perceptibility of petroglyphs and the minimum distance from the major pathways suggests, as expected, the existence of significant differences (Kruskal-

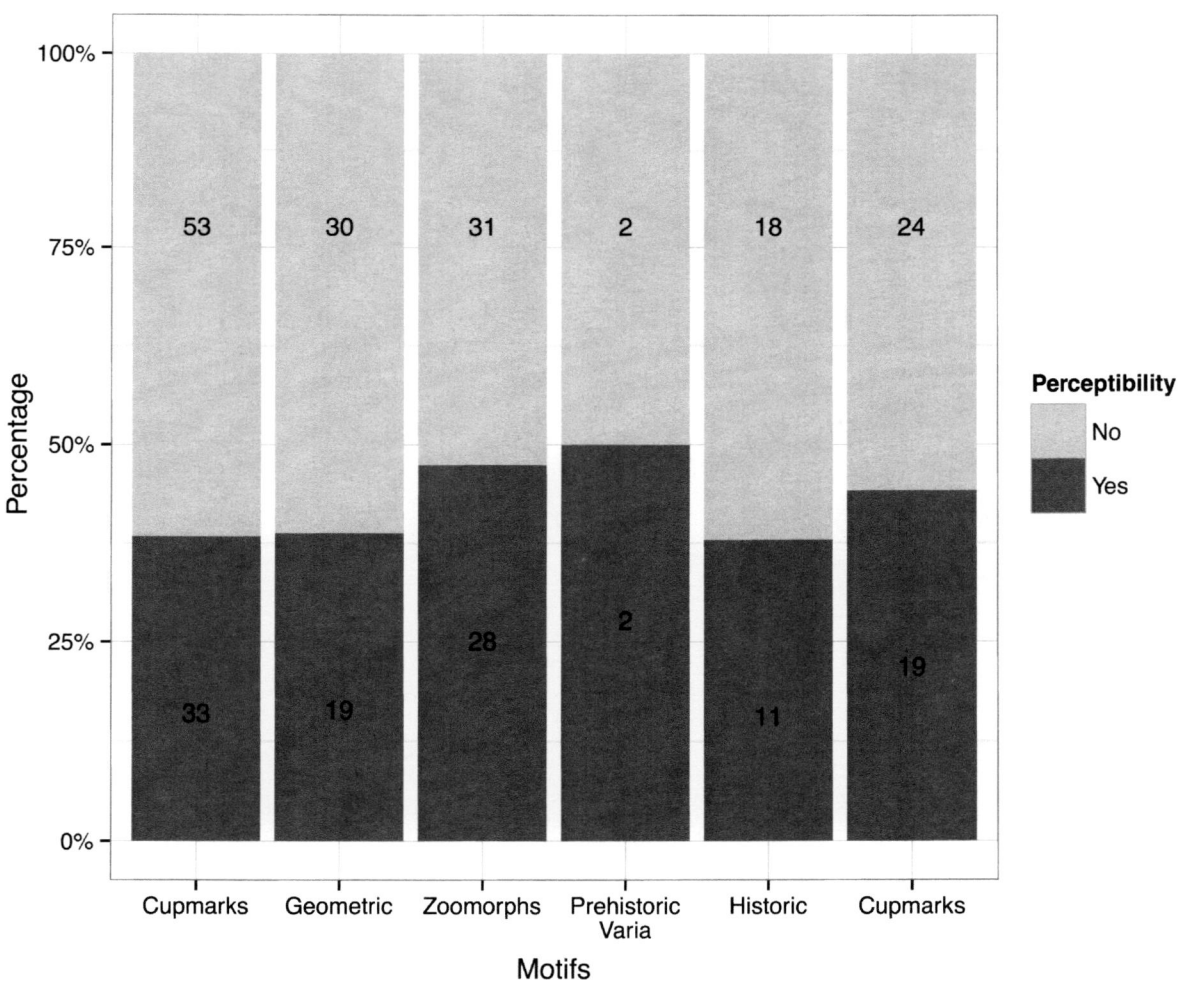

FIGURE 3. PERCENTAGE OF PETROGLYPHS PERCEIVED FROM THE MAJOR PATHWAYS CALCULATED USING GRASS GIS.

Wallis chi-squared = 81.4284, df = 1, p-value < 2.2e-16). Furthermore, the correlation analysis (Pearson's r) between both perceptibility and distance shows a negative result (-0.64), evidencing that the farther away a rock art site is from the major pathways, the lower the chances of it being noticed. This circumstance supports the traditional assumption of remoteness as a major method for the seclusion of open-air rock art (Bradley, 1997). However, although such correlation does exist, this is not very strong, suggesting that –besides distance– there may be other topographic factors that can also alter the perception of petroglyphs.

This circumstance can be easily observed in the fact that many of the rock art sites that were not perceived are close to major pathways (Figure 4). Thus, 24 (27.5%) of the 87 petroglyphs closer than 250 meters to these paths cannot be seen from them, even when some of these are located only 3 meters away.

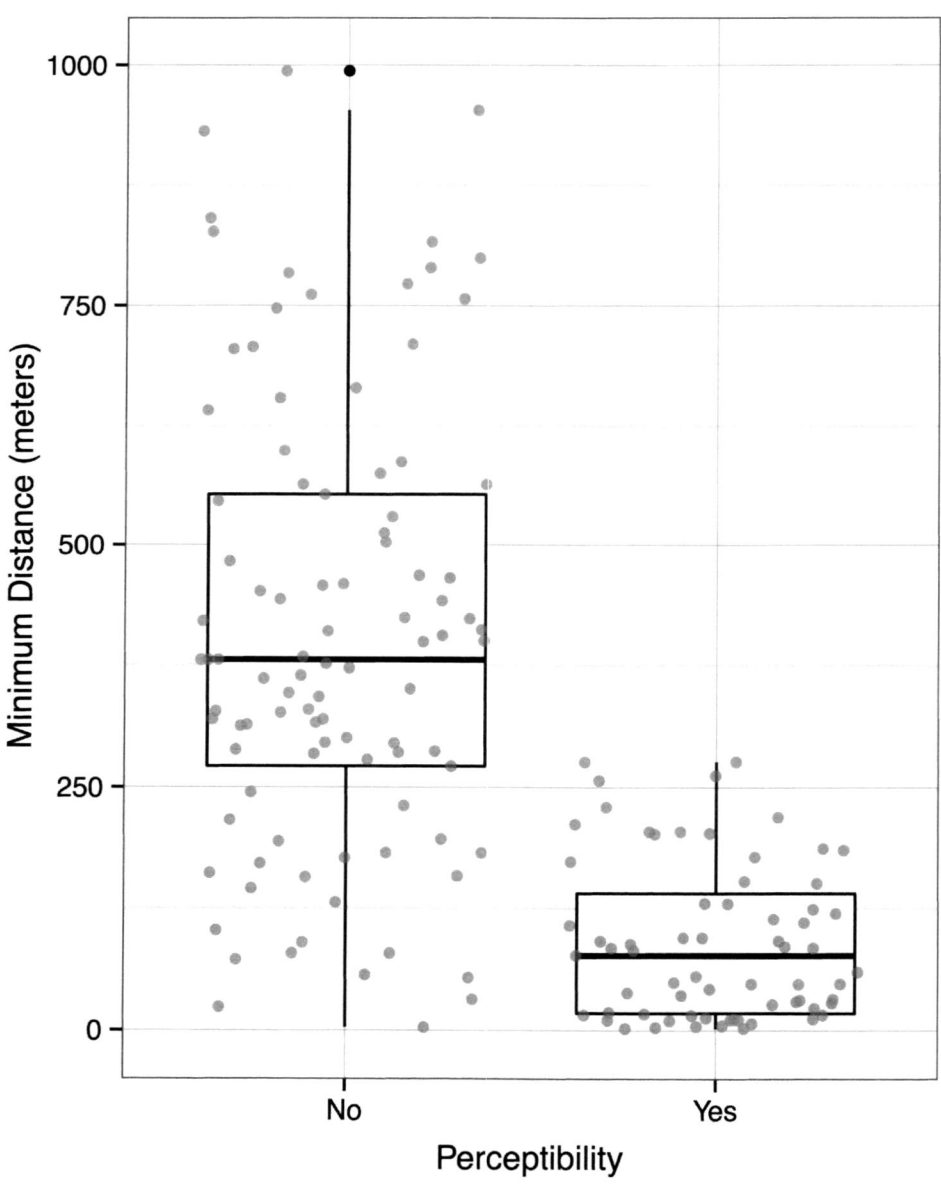

FIGURE 4. MINIMUM DISTANCE OF PETROGLYPHS THAT WERE AND WERE NOT PERCEIVED FROM THE MAJOR PATHWAYS.

5. Conclusions

The analysis of the relationship between the open-air rock art sites of Northern Barbanza Peninsula and the theoretically-defined major pathways across the landscape has shown how there is a spatial proximity between both (with a mean distance of only 300 meters), which might be used as a evidence for supporting the traditional hypothesis of Galician petroglyphs linked with routes across the landscape and with the so-called 'geography of movement'.

However, behind this *Euclidean* proximity there is a much more complex reality. Thus, a simple GIS analysis of the –usually forgotten– perceptibility of petroglyphs through 'inverse viewshed' suggests that even those rock art sites closer to major pathways could have gone totally unnoticed for individuals following them. Therefore, we should not automatically assume the spatial proximity of petroglyphs and paths as proof of a direct and unequivocal relationship. On the contrary, there are purely spatial factors that can isolate neighbouring areas and hide rock art sites located even in the vicinity of heavily transited places.

In conclusion, the traditional view of petroglyphs as mediators in the use of the landscape, acting as an intermediary and normative element of the land tenure among farmer groups begs for qualification. The automatic assumption of an open-air rock art easily noticeable and, therefore, accessible to everybody must take into account the possible existence of secluding measures that might have made engravings virtually invisible except for those people with a deep knowledge of the territory in which such elements are located. Some of these measures, such as those depending on the spatial location of rock art sites, can be easily analysed and studied.

Acknowledgments

The authors wish to thank Michael Barton and Isaac Ullah (School of Human Evolution and Social Change, Arizona State University) their help with the GRASS add-ons, especially *r.viewshed.cva.py*. The research leading to these results has received funding from the European Union's Seventh Framework Programme (FP7/2007-2013 – MSCA-COFUND) under grant agreement n°245743 – Post-doctoral programme Braudel-IFER-FMSH, in collaboration with the Laboratoire de Recherches Archéologiques (LARA) (CNRS, Université de Nantes).

References

Bradley, R. 1997. Rock art and the Prehistory of Atlantic Europe. London: Routledge.

Bradley, R. 2002. Access, style and imagery: the audience for prehistoric rock art in Atlantic Spain and Portugal, 4000-2000 BC. Oxford Journal of Archaeology. 21, p. 231-247.

Bradley, R.; Criado Boado, F.; Fábregas Valcarce, R. 1994. Los petroglifos como forma de apropiación del espacio: algunos ejemplos gallegos. Trabrajos de Prehistoria. 51, p. 159-168.

Brown, A. D.; Bradley, R.; Goldhahn, J.; Nord, J.; Skoglund, P.; Yendell, V. 2011. The environmental context of a prehistoric rock carving on the Bjäre Peninsula, Scania, southern Sweden. Journal of Archaeological Science. 38, p. 746-752.

Casimir, M. J. 1992. The determinants of rights to pasture: territorial organization and ecological constraints. In Casimir, M. J.; Rao, A., eds. – Mobility and Territoriality: Social and Spatial Boundaries among Foragers, Fishers, Pastoralists, and Peripatetics. New York: Berg, p. 153-203.

Criado Boado, F. 1999. Del Terreno al Espacio: planteamientos y perspectivas para la Arqueología del Paisaje. CAPA: cadernos de arqueoloxía e patrimonio, N° 6. Santiago de Compostela: Universidad de Santiago de Compostela.

Fábregas Valcarce, R. 2010. Os petróglifos e o seu contexto: un exemplo da Galicia meridional. Vigo: Insituto de Estudios Vigueses.

Fábregas Valcarce, R.; Rodríguez Rellán, C. 2012a. A arte rupestre do Norte da Península do Barbanza. In Fábregas Valcarce, R.; Rodríguez Rellán, C., eds. – A Arte Rupestre No Norte Do Barbanza. Santiago de Compostela: Andavira Editora, p. 61-84.

Fábregas Valcarce, R.; Rodríguez Rellán, C. 2012b. A Prehistoria Recente do Barbanza, In Fábregas Valcarce, R.; Rodríguez Rellán, C., eds. – A Arte Rupestre No Norte Do Barbanza. Santiago de Compostela: Andavira Editora, p. 85-106.

Fábregas Valcarce, R.; Rodríguez-Rellán, C. 2015. Walking on the stones of years. Some remarks on the NW Iberian rock art. In Ling, J.; Skoglund, P.; Bertilsson, U., eds. – Picturing the Bronze Age. Oxford: Oxbow Books, p. 47-63.

García Quintela, M. V.; Santos Estevez, M. 2004. Alineación arqueoastronómica en A Ferradura (Amoeiro-Ourense). Complutum. 15, p. 51-74.

Goldhahn, J.; Fuglestvedt, I.; Jones, A. 2013. Changing Pictures. An Introduction. In Goldhahn, J.; Fuglestvedt, I.; Jones, A., eds. – Changing Pictures. Rock Art Traditions and Visions in Northern Europe. Oxfod: Oxbow Books, p. 1-22.

Ingold, T. 1987. The appropriation of nature: essays on human ecology and social relations. Iowa City: University of Iowa Press.

Ling, J. 2006. Elevated rock art: maritime images and situations. Adoranten: årsskrift för Scandinavian Society for Prehistoric Art, Tanums hällristningsmuseum, p. 5-32.

Peña Santos, A. de la; Rey García, J. M. 2001. Petroglifos de Galicia. A Coruña: Vía Láctea.

Rodríguez Rellán, C.; Gorgoso López, L.; Fábregas Valcarce, R. 2008. O conxunto de petroglifos de Campo da Uz (Sta. María de Areas, Chantada) e as vías de tránsito cara o interior lucense. Gallaecia. 27, p. 35-61.

Santos Estévez, M.; Criado Boado, F. 1998. Espacios rupestres: del panel al paisaje. Arqueología Espacial. 19-20, p. 579-596.

Santos Estévez, M.; Criado Boado, F. 2000. Deconstructing rock art spatial grammar in the Galician Bronze Age. In Nash, G., ed. – Signifying Place and Space. World Perspectives of Rock Art and Landscapes. BAR International Series, 902. Oxford: Archaeopress.

Tilley, C. 2008. Body and Image: Explorations in landscape phenomenology 2. Walnut Creek: Left Coast Press.

Vázquez Martínez, A.; Fábregas Valcarce, R.; Rodríguez-Rellán, C. – Going by the numbers, a quantitative approach to the Galician prehistoric petroglyphs. This volume.

Villoch Vázquez, V. 1995. Monumentos y petroglifos: la construcción del espacio en las sociedades constructoras de túmulos del Noroeste peninsular. Trabajos de Prehistoria. 52, p. 39-55.

The paintings of "oculadas" figures in the Neolithic and Chalcolithic of Northern Portugal: the study case of Serra de Passos

Maria DE JESUS SANCHES
Faculty of Letters of Porto University;
Transdisciplinary "Culture, Space and Memory" Research Centre
mjsanches77@gmail.com

Abstract

The purpose of this paper is to make known 3 rock shelters / panels with very formalized images painted on them, known as "oculados" idols, discovered in Serra de Passos (Passos Mountain), northern Portugal. This is a region in which, until recently, these designs were unknown in the form of schematic painting.

These are figures and idiosyncratic compositions. Even though these show a certain resemblance to other southern and southeastern peninsular motifs, especially in the design of the eyes / eyebrows and facial tattoo, we will highlight its originality, this originality will be related with the specificity of the prehistoric settlement of Passos Mountain and its surroundings during the 3° mill. BC, as well as with the rise of socio political leaderships in the context of regional genealogical and iconographic traditions.

Keywords: *"oculados" idols; rock paintings; North of Portugal*

Résumé

L'objectif de cet article est de faire connaître trois abris sous roche/ panneaux comprenant des images peintes, très formalisées, connues comme des idoles "oculados", découverts dans la Serra de Passos, au nord du Portugal. C'est une région où, jusqu'à tout récemment, ces peintures préhistoriques étaient inconnus. Il s'agit de figures et de compositions totalement idiosyncrasiques. Bien que celles-ci montrent une certaine ressemblance à d'autres motifs du sud et du sud-ouest de la péninsule ibérique, en particulier dans la conception des yeux /sourcils et du tatouage facial, nous mettrons en évidence son originalité. Cette originalité sera liée à la spécificité du peuplement préhistorique de la Serra de Passos, de son environnement géographique au cours du 3ème millénaire AC, et à l'affirmation de leaderships socio-politiques dans le contexte des traditions généalogiques et iconographiques de cette région.

Mots-clés: *idole "oculado"; peinture rupestre; Nord du Portugal*

1. Introduction

Three rock shelters / panels from Regato das Bouças display "oculados" figures, also called "oculados" idols. These panels, identified in late 2010, are part of the most extensive concentration of rock shelters with schematic painting or of schematic tradition known to the present date in all Northwestern Iberia, which is precisely the Passos mountain area (Sanches, *et al.*, in press).

This mountain displays a minimum of 26 rock shelters that contain a total of more than six dozen panels.[1] Another set, also with enough scientific relevance, but a little more dispersed geographically, is being defined along the valley of the River Coa (Figueiredo & Baptista, 2013).

Scientific findings and studies in recent years have come to show that the Trás-os-Montes eastern region and the neighboring Beira Douro region, which are geographically and topographically in the continuity of the Iberian Meseta, hold more iconographic painted manifestations than previously

---

[1] A comprehensive study of the rock shelters of the Passos mountain, where decalcs and other records are shown, is being published in the journal of Estudos Pré-históricos (Sanches, *et al.*, in press).

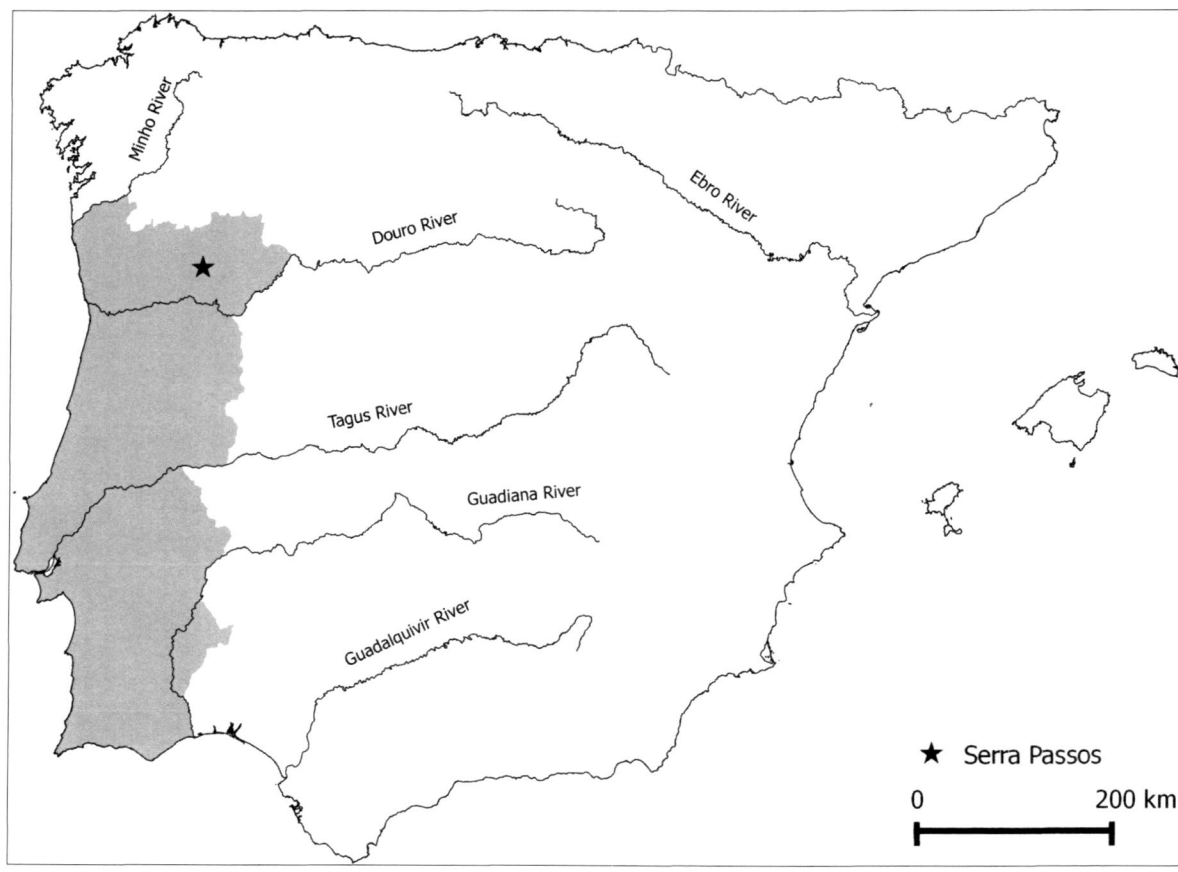

FIGURE 1. GEOGRAPHICAL LOCATION OF THE PASSOS MOUNTAIN (SERRA DE PASSOS) IN THE NORTH OF PORTUGAL (NORTHWEST IBERIA).

thought. Looking at the density of shelters published in this region (Zamora, León, Salamanca, Avila, Burgos, Soria, Palencia, Segovia) totaling 139 (Gómez-Barrera 2005), the present day aforementioned portuguese territory must be treated not as marginal, but as integrating part of that central Iberian unit.

Given that the rock shelters of the Passos Mountain are a part of a landscape that for long has been inhabited since at least the Neolithic to the Early Bronze Age (5th to late 3rd mill. BC) (Sanches 1997; 2002), on our approach emphasis will be given on the ways of inhabiting the territory, witnessed by archaeological contexts.

The painted motifs, and particularly the "oculadas" figures will be discussed as a means and object through which the local agro-pastoral communities establish, at the local and regional levels, inter-community and intra-community ties that revolve around leadership and competition for resources, particularly in agriculture.

2. Passos Mountain: rock shelters geographic and topographic context

We could approach the Passos mountain area (Trás-os-Montes/Northeast of Portugal) and their varied prehistoric places in multiple perspectives.

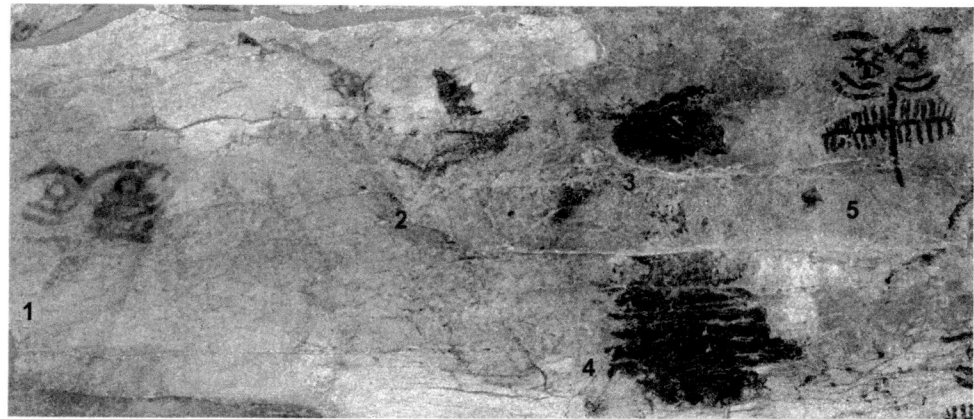
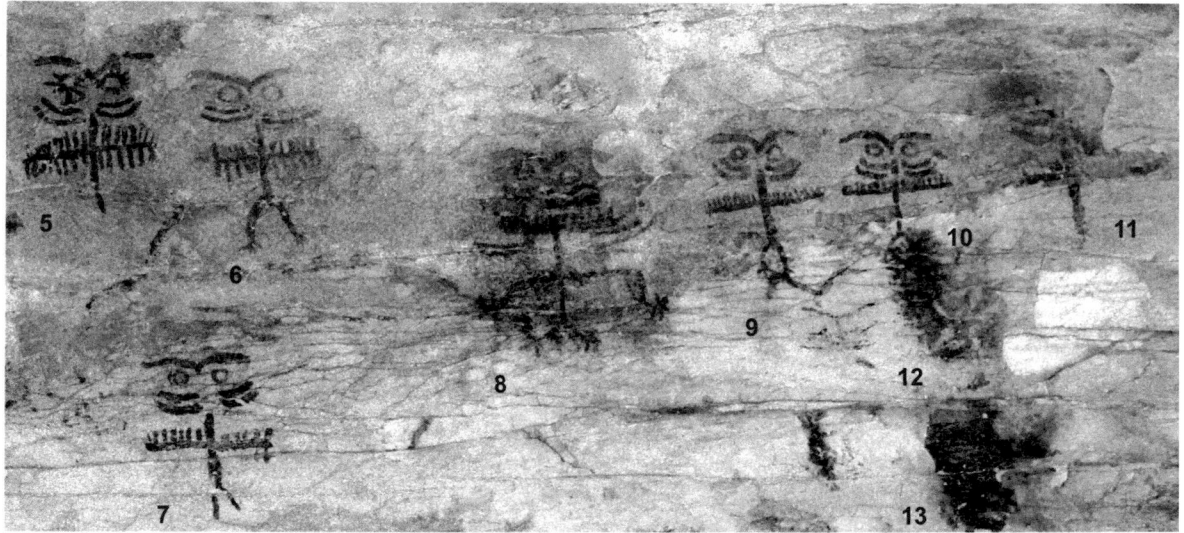

FIGURE 2. COMPOSITION OF "OCULADOS" IDOL-LIKE FIGURES (PAINTED RED), LOCATED ON THE TOP OF THE PANEL (ROCK SHELTER 11 OF REGATO DAS BOUÇAS). THIS IS A SINGLE IMAGE SPLIT IN TWO IN ORDER TO ADAPT TO THIS PUBLICATION, NOTE: MOTIF 5 IS REPEATED.

In fact, all of the archaeological, historical and ethnographic documentation requires us to observe this mountain both in a relation of complementarity and of economic specialization (and even religious specialization, through the Chapel of Santa Comba) with the lowlands that surround it. The mountain is a kind of "hill-island" that due to its altitude (500-1000 meters) dominates all the surrounding landscape. It is a physical and visual landmark in the regional landscape as it displays vigorous quartzite escarpments reliefs where natural rock shelters open up (with various shapes and sizes) and where natural panels that served as a pretext and context to prehistoric paintings are to be found (Sanches 2002; 2006).

The richness in water on all topographies of the mountain (springs and streams) is noteworthy, with a highlight, for the purposes of this text, that the rock shelters with schematic paintings are located on the main valleys that access the top of the mountain, where one can find the paradigmatic Buraco da Pala (to be discussed below). These are the streams of the valleys of Regato das Bouças, of Ribeira da Cabreira and of Ribeira da Pousada 2. However focusing only on natural accesses would be a superficial approach that is, focusing only on the easiest natural courses. Actually some rock shelters

/ panels located at high altitudes, especially those recently discovered in Pala escarpment (930 m) reveal archaeological realities difficult to grasp (Sanches *et al.*, in press). From the Escarpment of Pala, located in a culminating topography, one has a circular, absolute view over all the surrounding territory, including over Regato das Bouças itself. Additionally, the Regato das Bouças valley is the shortest and easiest natural route of access to the top of the mountain, where the Buraco da Pala rock shelter is located, a place with which these shelters closely relate as we will argue later.

In truth, the long period of prehistoric occupation of the Passos mountain and its peripheral region (Sanches 1997; 2002), leads us to admit that the intense collective life was accompanied by social, political and ideological manifestations, difficult to conceptualize in a simple manner. Thus, the paintings of the rock shelters 1, 11 and 15 (A and B) that exhibit anthropomorphic "oculados" idols (included in a global spatial context of predominantly geometric-abstract iconography of polysemic nature) certainly admit multiple interpretations according to the different angle approach.

3. The rock shelters with idol-like "oculados"

3.1. The rock shelters / panels displaying "oculados" idols

The rock shelters / panels displaying "oculados" idols are located, as stated, on the impressive cliffs of Regato das Bouças margins. This restricted area concentrates the largest number of rock shelters (18 shelters) across the Passos mountain, totaling a minimum of 60 panels and several hundred motifs.

Of these 18 we must highlight: a) rock shelter 3 (situated on the escarpment on the right bank), given its size, number of panels (27) and difficulty of access (through a perilous climb); b) rock-shelter 2 because it has three panels with anthropomorphic figures (the only recorded on the mountain if we exclude those with "oculados idols"); c) rock shelters 11, 15 A / B and 1 on the escarpment of the left bank because they contain almost exclusively anthropomorphic "oculados" motifs, portraying different configurations (Sanches *et al.*, in press).

These shelters / panels with oculados motifs occupy specific spaces within the escarpment at relative altitudes where one has extensive views of the area north and east of Mirandela basin. Thus, the figures are facing the exterior of the mountain, providing a visual dominance over an extended area. However, due to the steepness of the ground, which is very rugged, the presence of large audiences in front of the panels is impossible.

3.1.1. Rock shelter/panel 11 of Regato das Bouças

It is a large vertical quartzite panel, facing (approximately) the southwest. It seems to contain 18 motifs, all in red color, although the 13 that can be seen most clearly align themselves horizontally on top of the panel in a length of approximately 40 x 130 cm. On this upper set 9 figures are clearly "oculadas": 2 of them are reduced just to their faces ("eyes / eyebrows / tattoo") (Fig. 2: 2, 2) and 7 of them displaying "oculada" face and schematic body (Fig. 2: 5, 6, 7, 8, 9, 10, 11).[2] These are usually similar to each other but at the same time display differences that we believe should be valued.

A more careful observation of the panel makes it possible to see that in the upper part there is a dynamic composition formed by these whole-bodied "oculadas" figures. This composition focuses on a more complex figure provided with arms, five-fingered hands and feet (these with 3 fingers?) (Fig. 2: 8). Around this central figure, both from its left and right side, 3 figures and 2 spots show up respectively. Although there isn't symmetry in the literal sense of the term, there is a compositional symmetry as the similarities between the anthropomorphic motifs that are on both sides of idol-like figure nº 8 are undeniable. In fact, although motif nº 11 (Fig. 2) is quite destroyed, it does have the

---

[2] Figures 2 and 3 are spectral images by Luis Bravo Pereira.

same "eye design" of n° 5. In the remaining part of the body design both idol-like figures are the same.

Beneath color stain n° 4 (Fig. 2) there seems to have been a small idol-like face, that we believe was intentionally erased with paint of the same color (red), as we have evidence that this has happened in rock shelter 1.

By disregarding the erased figures, which would develop at the bottom of panel 11 (and that we cannot interpret), we can take a glimpse at the mythological and highly encrypted narrative whose meaning would correspond to a knowledge accessible and manageable only by a small social group. Some elements of a more naturalistic character such as, the "dancing" performance of figure 7, or the apparent serpent-like motif that figure 9 seems to hold between its feet (the claws of a bird of prey? a serpent ?) (Fig. 2: 7 and 9), reinforce the idiosyncrasy of this iconography that isn't at all similar with that of the remaining rock shelters of this mountain.

3.1.2. Rock shelter/panel 15 A and B of Regato das Bouças

Rock shelter 15 has a very peculiar configuration, consisting of two areas with paintings: A and B, given that A is overlooking B. It seems to us that they would be part of the same iconographic and symbolic set. Therefore we assume that the two figures from 15 A would act, from a spatial and compositional point of view, as guardians in relation to the entire 15 B panel. Panel 15 A is a rocky recess (shelter) located more than 2 m high, and difficult to climb to. It bears natural panels and on two of them, facing each other and simultaneously facing both the valley and the lowlands of the eastern part of the mountain, there are 2 idol-like complex figures (faces / masks?) displayed on Fig. 3: 1 and 2. Both of them are painted red. Note that although these "oculadas" faces both have the same general features, they are distinguishable as if in their design it had been absolutely necessary to iconographically point out that it was about two separate entities. The rocky protection allowed its excellent preservation.

Further below and now with easier access, panel 15 B is a large vertical surface scarcely protected by a small rocky outcrop. The percolation of water over the surface, and the poor state of conservation of the rock's surface, leads us to suppose that there would have existed a large number of figures there: perhaps a minimum of 20, of which 11 of the "oculadas" kind. The preserved part, particularly in the upper sector, leads us to believe that an extensive composition could have been painted there. Indeed, 3 diagonally aligned motives are framed by elongated spots (Fig. 3: 3, 4) and at the same time surrounded by 5 "oculados" motifs (3 of these are in Fig. 3: 5, 6 and 7).

The lower right sector of the panel is very destroyed, although one can glimpse a few figures there. We should highlight an idol-like "oculada" figure (distinct from all others), and also a spot that seems to correspond to an intentional paint over an "oculada" figure (deletion by red paint). Likewise in this rock shelter / panel B the figures aren't exactly the same between themselves. They share, however, in some cases the circle-like eyes or radiated circles; in other, facial tattoos and / or a sort of head ornament on top.

The figures portrayed on rock shelter 15 seem to be much more elaborate and complex than those on panel 11 and, as such, a much more detailed technical and symbolic knowledge was required to make them. This is really an extremely specialized painting, corresponding, as in the previous rock shelter, to knowledges and techniques only accessible to restricted community members whose status and social role was decisive in community and perhaps even intra-community cohesion.

3.1.3. Rock shelter 1 of Regato das Bouças

Number 1 is a rock shelter underneath the rock in the literal sense of the term. And, as stated, from it one dominates the eastern part of Mirandela basin. It is at the entrance wall on the left side where

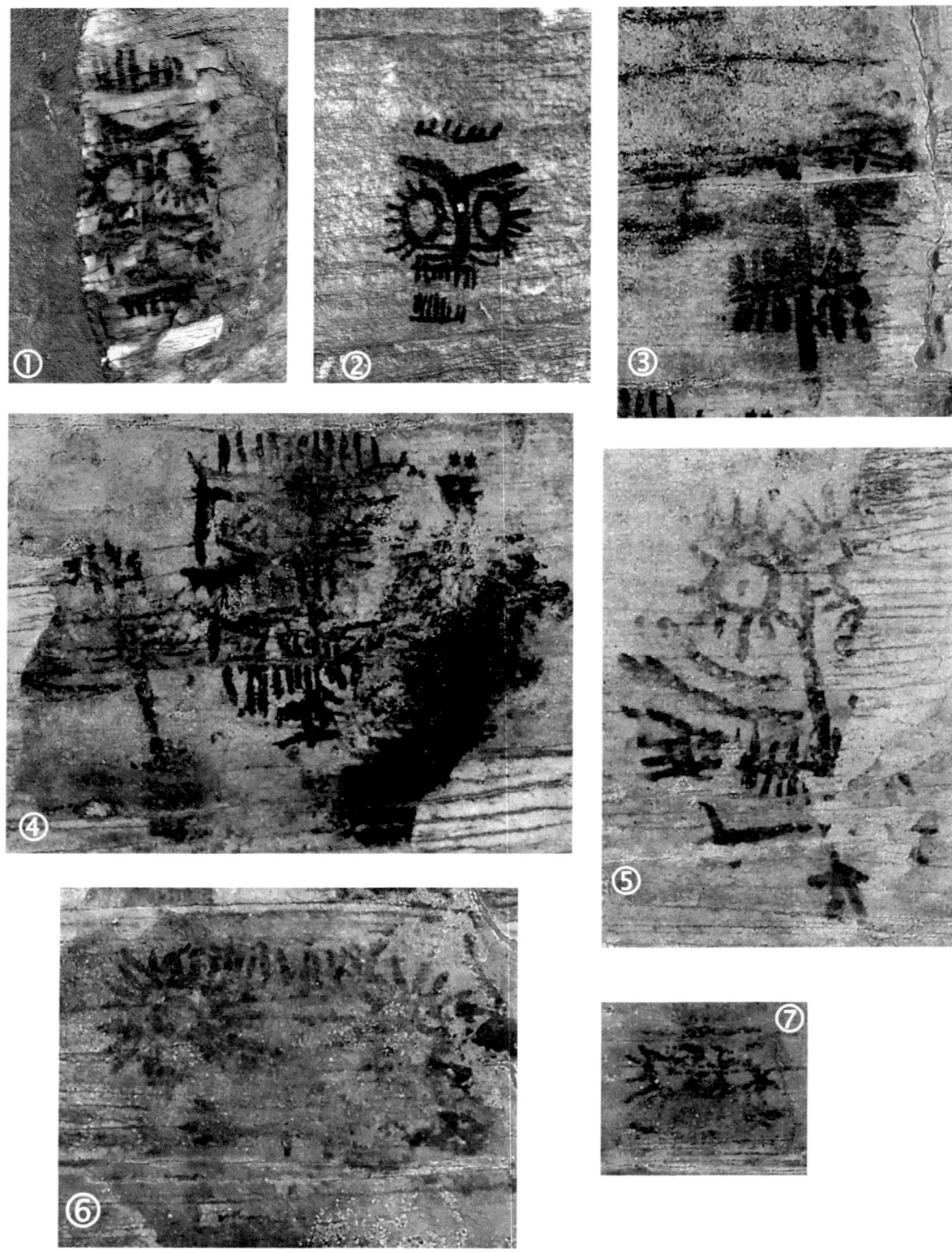

FIGURE 3. "OCULADOS" IDOL-LIKE FIGURES (PAINTED RED) FROM ROCKSHELTER 15 A (Nº 1 AND 2) AND 15 B (Nº 3, 4, 5, 6, 7) (REGATO DAS BOUÇAS).

a vertical panel with very deteriorated motifs can be found. At the top of the panel we have a red colored stain that is clearly the end product of repainting, or painting over, a "oculada" face. Beneath this figure we can also find a traditional motif composed of vertical parallel lines.

4. Discussion

In other texts the iconographic motifs of the Serra de Passos' rock shelters were discussed. However it is interesting to point out here that the majority, or almost all of them, are geometric and abstract, therefore absolutely distinct from those belonging to the panels with "oculados" idol-like figures described above (Sanches 2006; Sanches *et al.*, in press).

The *arboriformes* (tree-like motifs), *pectiformes* (comb-like motifs) or solar / radiated figures are the iconographic elements with which some "oculados idols" were conceived. These are common motifs in Schematic Art (particularly in rock shelter painting) and, as other authors have pointed out, also in Iberian megalithic art. However, the originality of the compositions and the complexity of the "oculadas" idol-like figures that integrate them are the most peculiar aspects of the rock shelters of Regato das Bouças (Fig. 2; 3).

The motifs with which we are concerned all have, overall, an anthropomorphic character, closely relatable from an iconographic point of view with a wide range of representations known as "oculados idols" in mobile art from the recent Prehistory (cylinder-idols, plaque-idols, idols on phalanx and idols on long bones,) which are found in various domestic and burial contexts, especially in the southern half of the Iberian Peninsula (Hurtado 2010; Bueno 2010).The decoration of ceramic vessels is another expression of this imagery (Ruiz López 2006; Fabián 2006; Jorge 1986; 2004), but because these vessels are in our regional context they will be approached later on. Actually, in painting, these motifs are not that frequent (Acosta 1968), being mostly found in the southern half of the Iberian Peninsula. Having said this they can also be found in the Northern Meseta / Douro Valley, where, after all, they are relatively rare (Gómez-Barrera 2005; Ruiz López 2006; Ruiz López *et al.* 2012).

It is not the purpose of this paper to look for the typologies and contexts of the forms / peninsular representations of "oculados idols". It is however to find a first comprehensive explanation of regional and global character for this kind of images of Passos mountain, since we believe that it is in the local and regional contexts that the first step towards understanding the extent of the behavior of the prehistoric communities must be made.

As Gomez-Barrera has pointed out (2005: 36), referring to the schematic painting of the Iberian Meseta, it always has common elements or shared elements between sites. However, side by side with these often we find individualizing elements that would point out the concrete material and social conditions that the panels would give meaning to. Moreover, the same author argues that even inside painting "schematism" it is possible, in many cases, to individualize narratives, particularly in the rock shelters of Soria (Gomez-Barrera 2005: 37-38). On the other hand, the anthropological concept of "agency" (Gell 1998) precisely calls for that active intervention of the community (or group of communities linked by kinship) in the transformation and justification of the cosmogonic principles that govern it, given that the images are used as active elements of those modifications. In Regato das Bouças 11, 15 A / B the high cast of "oculadas entities" and its formal diversity (masks? banners? deities?) also calls for the emergence of new genealogical narratives. These constitute breaches in relations between the different communities and in their relationship with the land, in a period that began at the end of the 4th millennium but gained a greater regional expression during the 3rd mill. BC.

This interpretation rests, naturally, in the absolute chronology and nature of the excavated contexts in Passos Mountain and its surrounding lowlands, dated between the 5th-3rd mill. BC.

Given that we are dealing with published documentation, we will focus only on the points that we consider essential.

Since the 5th millennium BC that Passos mountain has Neolithic occupations of a seasonal character in Buraco da Pala rock shelter (and probably in other rock shelters too); moreover it is accepted by most researchers that at least since the beginning of the 4th mill. BC the cultivation of cereals and *Leguminosae* is proven in this mountain (Sanches 1997). Whether in the mountain or in the lowlands that surround it the anthracologic studies of megalithic monuments indicate that regional ecosystems are under agricultural and / or pastoral pressure in the 4th millennium BC (Figueiral & Sanches, 2003; Sanches *et al*. 2007), and reveal a gradual creation of identitarian territories linked to the ancestors. It is noteworthy that in some of these megalithic monuments images common to those of schematic painting are to be found — Mamoa do Castelo (Sanches 2002) and Madorras (Gonçalves and Cruz 1994) — as well as *stelae* where the configuration of the face is reduced to its simplest expression. A global iconographic and stratigraphic analysis of the schematic painting of Passos mountain, published in other papers (Sanches 1997; 2002), led us to argue that the oldest establishment of places and paths in Passos mountain — also defined by the location of painted rock shelters — would date from the late 5th to all throughout the 4th millennium BC.

During this period as well as the 3th mill BC, collective life would establish a relation of complementarity between the mountains and the lowlands, although the "roles" of both areas in economic and social life appear to have varied over time.

According to Susana Jorge (1999b: 67) it is at the turn of the 4th to the 3rd millennium BC, and during the latter, that the first agro-pastoral landscape in Portuguese territory is accomplished, although this landscape integrates a wide range of very heterogeneous social spaces where the power of the first undeniably agrarian societies is negotiated, opinion with which we agree.

The results of regional excavations sites — as those of Buraco da Pala, *stelae* precincts of Cabeço da Mina (Vila Flor) (Jorge 1999a; Sanches 2010) and monumental precincts of Crasto de Palheiros-Murça (Sanches & Pinto 2008), Castelo Velho de Freixo de Numão (Foz Côa) (Jorge 2004) and of S. Lourenço (Chaves) (Jorge 1986) — are consistent with that interpretation. We should highlight that two of them are located in the Passos mountain area: Buraco da Pala at the top and Crasto de Palheiros in the southern lowlands of that mountain.

Thus, we must turn back again to the Buraco da Pala rock shelter and to its storage levels (barn) I and II, dating between 2800 and 2500 BC. Here, at the level I, a ceramic vase with "oculada" decoration (Fig. 4) was found which provides an approximate chronology for rock shelters 11, 15 A / B and 1 of Regato das Bouças. Simultaneously this vase demonstrates that there is a "motif-idea" which closely and ideologically connects the two contexts: the storage level I of Buraco da Pala and the idol-like "oculadas" figures of Regato das Bouças.

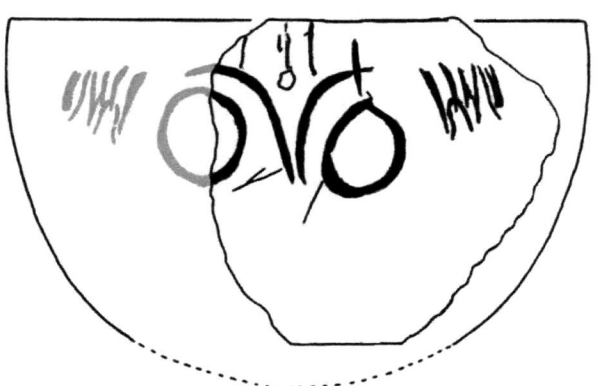

FIGURE 4. CERAMIC VASE WITH "OCULADA" DECORATION, FOUND IN LEVEL I OF BURACO DA PALA ROCK SHELTER.

Both at level I and II of Buraco da Pala there are two distinct "functional" areas: one of consumption and another of storage. The consumption area is considerably reduced from its older level (level II) to its most recent one (level I).[3] Storage characteristics, composed by huge quantities of products

---

[3] Stratigraphy shows that level I is more recent than level II, carbon dating however doesn't allow us to establish that chronological distinction.

obtained mainly through agriculture (fava beans, barley, wheat) and gathering (acorn) indicates that such products held a remarkable value in this communities' economy. These products were found carbonized (Sanches 1997).

However, its destruction by fire, accompanied by the non-removal of the vases / containers and their burnt content, can be interpreted as an intention to "preserve" a symbolic value since these products are no longer usable as food. At the same time, it appears that in a restricted area of the rock shelter other products have been consumed in addition to the stored products: opium poppy seeds, lentils, peas and linseed (flax).

It should also be noted that there were 3 successive recorded "fires" without any removal of its remains — two "fires" in level II and 1 in level I. Therefore the intention of preserving the burned products in this rock shelter seems clear to us.

The exceptional nature of the uses of Buraco da Pala at its storage / fire levels, and particularly in level I — given that the barn occupies most of the available area —, is also documented by the absence of sufficient instruments relating to routine activities. On the other hand, gold and variscite ornaments and copper utensils can be found there. All things considered, we are led to interpret the Buraco da Pala rock shelter during the first half of the 3rd mill. BC as a place of collective negotiation between regional leaders under the context of competition and creation of land rights, where rituals linked to consumption, exchange and destruction (of potlatch kind) could take place.

As mentioned above, the chronology of the creation of the panels with "oculados" idol-like figures from Regato das Bouças will be the same as that of the vase found in Buraco da Pala (Fig. 4). Although we are unaware of the chronology of the 3 painted panels of this last rock shelter, it is likely that from the first half of the 3rd millennium BC its "content" was understood as "forbidden", and its social access even more restricted. Perhaps Regato das Bouças, which concentrates a very high number of rock shelters, panels and figures — some of which dateable from at least the 4th mill. BC — came to be used during the 3rd mill. BC as a place of ideological connection between the past, tradition and change, similarly to Buraco da Pala.

While we know that the "oculadas" idol-like figures, in the form of painting or mobile artefacts, have peninsular chronologies starting from the 5th mill. BC — as is the case of the paintings and ceramic vase of the Cueva de Los Murciélagos of Zuheros (Gavilán & Mas 2006) — or dating from the early 4th mill BC, as is the case of Abrigo de los Oculados, Cuenca (Ruiz López, *et al.* 2012), we will admit a regional chronology within the Chalcolithic. Besides the dates from Buraco da Pala rock shelter we have vases with very standardized "oculadas" decoration, also dated from the 3rd mill. BC in the monumental precincts of Castelo Velho Freixo de Numão (Foz Coa) (Jorge 2004) and S. Lourenço (Chaves) (Jorge 1986)

In short, this imagery is, after all, very rare in the northern half of Iberia whatever the archaeological context is. This exceptionality also links itself, during the 3rd mill. BC, with very complex archaeological sites, bearing great variability of architectonic structures and archaeological materials. This diversity demands anthropological and archaeological regional studies without which we can't understand these pre-historic communities that seem to be so incomprehensible to us.

Acknowledgements

I would like to thank João Francisco S. C. Sanches for the translation of this text to English.

Bibliography

Acosta, P. 1968. *La Pintura Rupestre Esquemática en España*. Salamanca: Universidad de Salamanca.

Bueno Ramirez, P. 2010. Ancestros e imágenes antropomorfas muebles en el ámbito del megalitismo occidental: las placas decoradas. In C. Cacho, M. R., E. Galán, & J. Martos, *Ojos que nunca se cierram. Ídolos en las primeras sociedades campesinas*. Madrid: Museo Arqueologico Nacional, pp. 39-77.

Fabián García, F. 2006. *El IV y el III Milenio AC en el Valle Amblés (Ávila). Arqueologia de Castilla y León* – Série de Monografias (Vol. 5). Salamanca: Junta de Castilla e León.

Figueiral, I.; Sanches, M. J.; Figueiral, I. 2003. Eastern Trás-os-Montes (NE Portugal) from the late Prehistory to the Iron age: the land and the people. In Fouache, E. (ed.), *The Mediterranean World Environment and History*. Elsevier, pp. 315-329.

Figueiredo, S. & Baptista, A. 2013. A arte esquemática pintada em Portugal. In J. Martinez Garcia & M. S. Hernández Pérez (eds.), *Actas del Congreso de Arte Rupestre en la Península Ibérica:comarca de Los Vélez*, pp. 301-315.

Gell, A. 1998. *Art and Agency. An Anthropological Theory*. Oxford. Clarendon Press.

Gavilán, B. & Mas, M. 2006. La Cueva de los Murciélagos de Zuheros (Córdoba): hábitat y santuário durante el neolítico antiguo. Hogares, *papaver somniferum* y simbolismo. *SPAL*, 15, pp. 21-37.

Gavilán, B. & Escacena, J. L. 2009. Acerca del primero neolitico de Aldalucia occidental. Los tramos medio y bajo de la cuenca del Guadalquivir. *Mainake, XXXI*, pp. 311-351.

Gómez-Barrera, J. A. 2005. La pintura esquemática como acción social de los grupos agro-ganaderos en la meseta castellano-leonesa. *Cuadernos de Arte Rupestre*, 2, pp. 11-58.

Gonçalves, A. H. & Cruz, D. J. 1994. Resultados do trabalho de escavação da Mamoa 1 de Madorras (S. Lourença de Ribapinhão, Sabrosa, Vila Real). *Estudos Pré-históricos, 2*, pp. 171-231.

Hurtado, V. 2010. Representaciones simbólicas, sítios, contextos e identidades territoriales en el suroeste peninsular. In C. Cacho, M. R. E. Galán, & J. Martos, *Ojos que nunca se cierram. Ídolos en las primeras sociedades campesinas*. Madrid: Museo Arqueologico Nacional, pp. 137-197.

Jorge, S. O. 1986. *Povoados da Pré-história Recente (IIIº-inícios do IIº milénio A.C.) da região de Chaves-Vila Pouca de Aguiar (Trás-os-Montes Ocidental)* (Vols. Ia, Ib e II). Porto: Instituto de Arqueologia da FLUP.

Jorge, S. O. 1999a. Stéles et statues-menhires de l'Age du Bronze de la Péninsule Ibérique:discours de pouvoir. *L'Europe au Temps d'Ulisses. Dieux et Héros de l'Âge du Bronze, 25. Exposition de l'art du Conseuil de la Europe* AFAA, pp. 114-122.

Jorge, S. O. 1999b. *Domesticar a Terra*. Gradiva.

Jorge, S. O. 2004. O sítio como mediador de sentido. Castelo Velho de Freixo de Numão: um recinto monumental pré-histórico do Norte de Portugal. In *Estudos de Homenagem a Luis de Oliveira Ramos*. Porto. FLUP, pp. 583-611.

Ruiz Lopes, J. F. 2006. El Abrigo de los Oculados (Henarejos, Cuenca). In J. Martinez Garcia & M. S. Hernández Pérez (eds.), *Actas del Congreso de Arte Rupestre en la Península Ibérica:comarca de Los Vélez*, pp. 375-386.

Ruiz López, J. F.; Hernandez, A.; Armitage, R.; Rowe, M.; Viñas, R.; Gavira-Vallejo, J. 2012. Calcium oxalate AMS 14C dating and chronology of post-Palaeolithic rock paintings in the Iberian peninsula. Two dates from Abrigo de los Oculados (Henarejos, Cuenca, Spain). *Journal of Archaeological Science*, 39, pp. 2655-2667.

Sanches, M. J. 1997. *Pré-história Recente de Trás-os-Montes e Alto Douro (Vol. I e II)*. Porto: Sociedade Portuguesa de Antropologia e Etnologia.

Sanches, M. J. 2002. Spaces for social representation, choreographic spaces and paths in the Serra de Passos and surrounding lowlands (Trás-os-Montes, Northern Portugal) in late prehistory. *Arkeos, 12, CEIPHAR*, pp. 65-105.

Sanches, M. J. 2006. Abrigos com pintura rupestre esquemática da Serra de Passos/Sta Comba [caixa inserta no cap. III]. In C. A. Brochado de Almeida (coord.), *História do Douro, 1*. Porto: GEHVID, pp. 126-129.

Sanches, M. J. 2010. As estelas antropomórficas de Picote-Miranda do Douro (Trás-os-Montes). In R. Vilaça (ed.), *IV Jornadas Raianas "Estelas e Estátuas-menires da Pré à Proto-história"*, C. M. Sabugal, CEAUCP e Instituto de Arqueologia do DHAA da FLUC. Sabugal, pp. 145-174.

SANCHES, M. J.; NUNES, S. A. e PINTO, D. P. 2007. Trás-os-Montes (Norte de Portugal) – As gentes e os ecossistemas, do Neolítico à Idade do Ferro. In S. O. Jorge, A. M. S. Bettencourt e I. Figueiral (eds.)- *A concepção das paisagens e dos espaços na Arqueologia da Península Ibérica* (Atas do 4º Congresso de Arqueologia Peninsular), Faro, pp. 189-206.

SANCHES, M. J. & PINTO, D. B. 2008. The architectural transformation of the Fragada do Crasto, or Crasto de Palheiros, from the beginning of the 3rd Millenium BC to the beginning of the 2nd century AD. In M. J. Sanches (ed.), *O Crasto de Palheiros (Fragada do Crasto), Murça-Portugal*. Município de Murça, Murça, pp. 21-38.

SANCHES, M. J.; MORAIS, P. R. e TEIXEIRA, J. C. 2013, (*in press*). Escarpas rochosas e pinturas na Serra de Passos/Sta Comba (Nordeste de Portugal) (Rock Escarpments and its schematic paintings in Passos/Sta Comba Mountain (Northeast of Portugal). In *Atas da II^a Mesa Redonda Artes Rupestres da Pré-história à Proto-história. (Estudos Pré-históricos*, 18) CEPBA.

Going by the numbers, a quantitative approach to the Galician prehistoric petroglyphs

Alia VÁZQUEZ MARTÍNEZ, Ramón FÁBREGAS VALCARCE
and Carlos RODRÍGUEZ-RELLÁN

GEPN – Departamento de Historia I. Facultade de Xeografía e Historia,
Universidade de Santiago de Compostela, Praza da Universidade, 1. 15782,
Santiago de Compostela, Spain

Abstract

Today, despite the notable progress on the knowledge about Galician carvings, we still lack an updated census of these and, as a result, we do not have adequate information about the precise number or the geographical distribution of the main groups of motifs that make up this artistic phenomenon. In order to tackle this problem, we have gone through the Xunta de Galicia's Catalogue of the Archaeological Heritage, obtaining a database of 3361 petroglyphs.

Keywords: *rock art, Galicia, GIS, geographical distribution*

Resumen

Hoy en día, a pesar del notable progreso en el conocimiento de los petroglifos gallegos, aun no disponemos de un censo actualizado de estas manifestaciones y, como resultado, tampoco tenemos una información adecuada en lo referente al número y distribución geográfica de los grupos de motivos que conforman este fenómeno artístico. Con el objetivo de abordar este problema, hemos inspeccionado el inventario de la Dirección Xeral de Patrimonio Cultural de la Xunta de Galicia, reuniendo una base de datos de 3361 petroglifos.

Palabras clave: *arte rupestre, Galicia, SIG, distribución geográfica*

State of the art

The references about the rock art in the Northwest part of the Iberian Peninsula were made over a hundred years ago. Since then, there has been an intense work of searching, documentation and diffusion of the complex rock art. This caused a rise in the publication of studies, written by local archaeologists, amateurs and even foreign professionals such as Anati or H. Obermaier. Despite all these works, the cataloguing process of this phenomenon was surprisingly limited, while it is true that the catalogue has been progressively increasing throughout the years.

The first references in historiography about Galician rock art are present in travel records around Galicia (Martín Sarmiento, 1745; Martínez Salazar, 1898; Murguía, 1865). The creation of a corpus of Galician petroglyphs was not started until the 19th century. It was carried out by the Archaeological Society of Pontevedra, where Enrique Campo Sobrino catalogued and draw almost 20 petroglyphs (San Ildefonso Rodríguez and Tilve Jar, 1995). During these years, there also appeared essays that described new findings. Those essays cannot be considered part of the cataloguing process, though they were of great value for Buhigas, who made an inventory of 250 engravings in the province of Pontevedra (Sobrino Buhigas, 1935).

In terms of numbers, the evolution of the petroglyph census in Galicia was not synchronous in the whole Galician territory throughout the past years. In fact, it was determined by the strong petroglyph search that took place in the province of Pontevedra, which ended up with 400 new entries in the corpus during the 1980s (García and Peña, 1980). Outside this province, there was a lack of quantitative

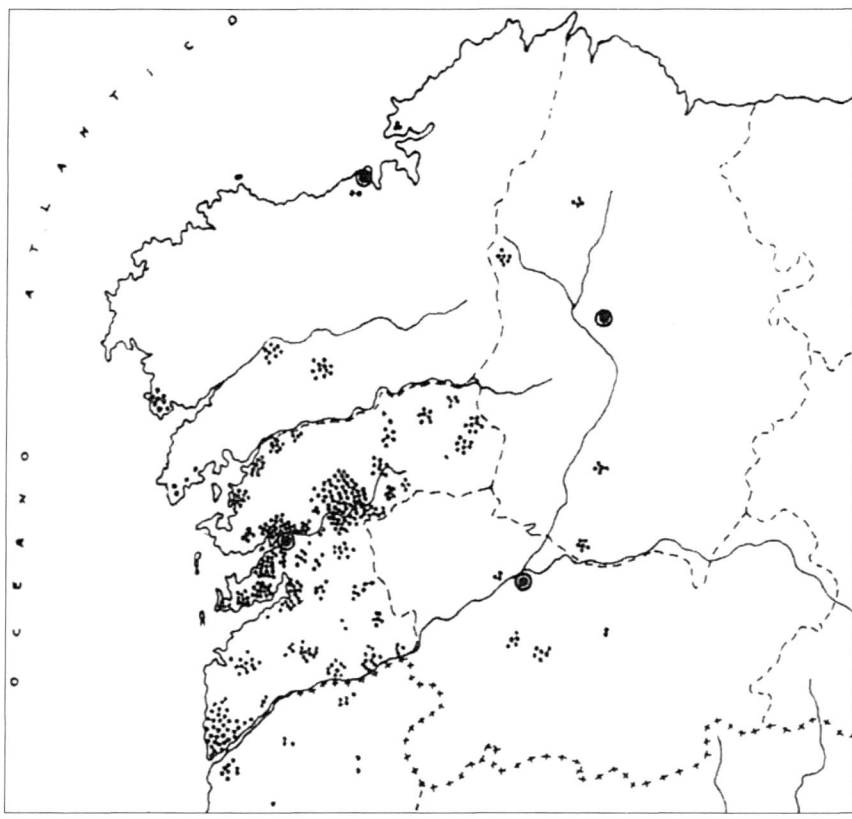

FIGURE 1. STATE OF THE KNOWLEDGE ABOUT THE DISTRIBUTION OF ROCK ART IN GALICIA (PEÑA AND VÁZQUEZ, 1979: 10).

works until the 21th century, when different authors published an essay with 154 items after a large bibliographic research (Barandela and Lorenzo, 2004), or the recent essays focused on the North of Barbanza (A Coruña) where have been catalogued 167 items in the recent years (Fábregas and Rodríguez, 2012). However, this still implies a partial record of the Galician petroglyphs we already know. Consequently, these cataloguing efforts are not only made because of the necessity of having a complete record of the rock engravings, but also to have a basis for the analysis of this phenomenon. A complete and definitive register allows us to know the relations between the rocks and their spatial disposition in Galicia.

Until the end of the 1970s, we did not have a map of the petroglyph distribution in Galicia (Varela, 1979). It is mainly focused in the Southwest of Galicia, especially around the Vigo and Pontevedra estuaries and with a greater density in the margins of the Lérez River –now considered to be the capital for rock art–. An important part of this distribution is conditioned by local researches, as suggested by the high number of rock art found in the coast.

After the initial systematic registers of petroglyphs that took place in the province of Pontevedra, the researchers considered that this data could be treated statistically. This idea originated the statistical essays that have been published on this topic. The association between the motifs in rock art was analysed through the 400 items registered by Peña and Rey García using the technique of Cluster analysis (Cancela Rey, *et al.* 1984). Before this research, the relation between the circular figures and deer was also studied, the first one using the linear regression technique (Cabaleiro Manzanedo, *et alii*, 1976) and the second one with a descriptive approach (García and Peña, 1980), both with a more limited number of engravings. The most complete research from those initial essays applying statistics to rock art is Cancela *et al.* (1984).

Methodology and materials

During 2013, the archaeological sites inscribed in the archaeological heritage catalogue of the Dirección Xeral de Patrimonio Cultural of the Xunta de Galicia were studied. This process allowed us to know the complete petroglyph census of Galicia, which consists of 3361 rock engravings.

In the first part of our research, this catalogue was only a limitation for the creation of a complete census, as it was not specifically designed to record the petroglyphs. It is rather a catalogue for every archaeological site than a rock art oriented database as the ones suggested by Carrera (1996) and Seoane (2009). This limitation affects all the engravings because they are not inventoried with detail. However, other problems have appeared: as the List of Archaeological sites has been built up over decades, it was written by several archaeologists. Thus, the information is variable due to the diversity of approaches, which provokes a lack of unanimity in this register.

The inventory obtained was subsequently analysed using Geographic Information Systems (Grass GIS) and data management programs. These have been used to draw a series of maps and charts to show the iconographic variability of the engraved panels, the correlation between motifs and their spatial distribution in Galicia.

Results

The increasing number of new findings of archaeological sites in Galicia was very significant throughout the history. However, those researches have been focused on the Southwestern area of Galicia, and this makes researchers think of this phenomenon as something limited to the Rías Baixas.

This hindered carrying out quantitative studies of the number of engravings in the Galician territory. Three decades ago (García and Peña, 1980), there was an initiative to count as many rock engravings as possible, but they only identified 400 units. In the map published by Peña and Vázquez (1979) it can be found the limited number of petroglyphs found in the other provinces, which reinforced the fragmentary vision of this phenomenon we have nowadays, centred in the Rías Baixas.

The article written by Vázquez Rozas (2006) is the first research that brings us closer to a statistical approximation of the petroglyphs in Galicia. However, the database of 1006 petroglyphs he used in this research was not recent, so it was probably out of date when he published this work (Vázquez Rozas, 1997).

Our research confirmed the tendency about the main sites Peña Santos and Vázquez Varela wrote about (1979) and Richard Bradley (1997: 165). The coastal areas (Figure 2), especially the province of Pontevedra and in particular the Rías Baixas –as it can be observed in the map– is the one with a wider number of engravings (1973 out of 3361 in Pontevedra). A Coruña (781 out of 3361) was studied in the recent years by amateurs and professional archaeologists (Fábregas and Rodríguez, 2012; Grupo de Arqueoloxía da Terra de Trasancos, 2009, 2011). This promoted the study of new rock art sites that were ignored, such as the northern area of Barbanza or the Vilarmaior town (Rodríguez and Fábregas, 2013).

The inland part of Galicia has a lower density of archaeological sites. After the research made in the province of Ourense in 2004 (Barandela and Lorenzo, 2004), focused on the creation of a written record of all the petroglyphs known through bibliographical notes, we could prove the increase of archaeological sites known in this province. In the last decade there were discovered 247 petroglyphs besides the 157 studied by Barandela and Lorenzo, which make a total of 404 out of 3361.

In the Northeastern area of Galicia (Lugo) the reduced number of archaeological sites with rock engravings is surprising. We registered 202 petroglyphs in Lugo, which show an increasing number

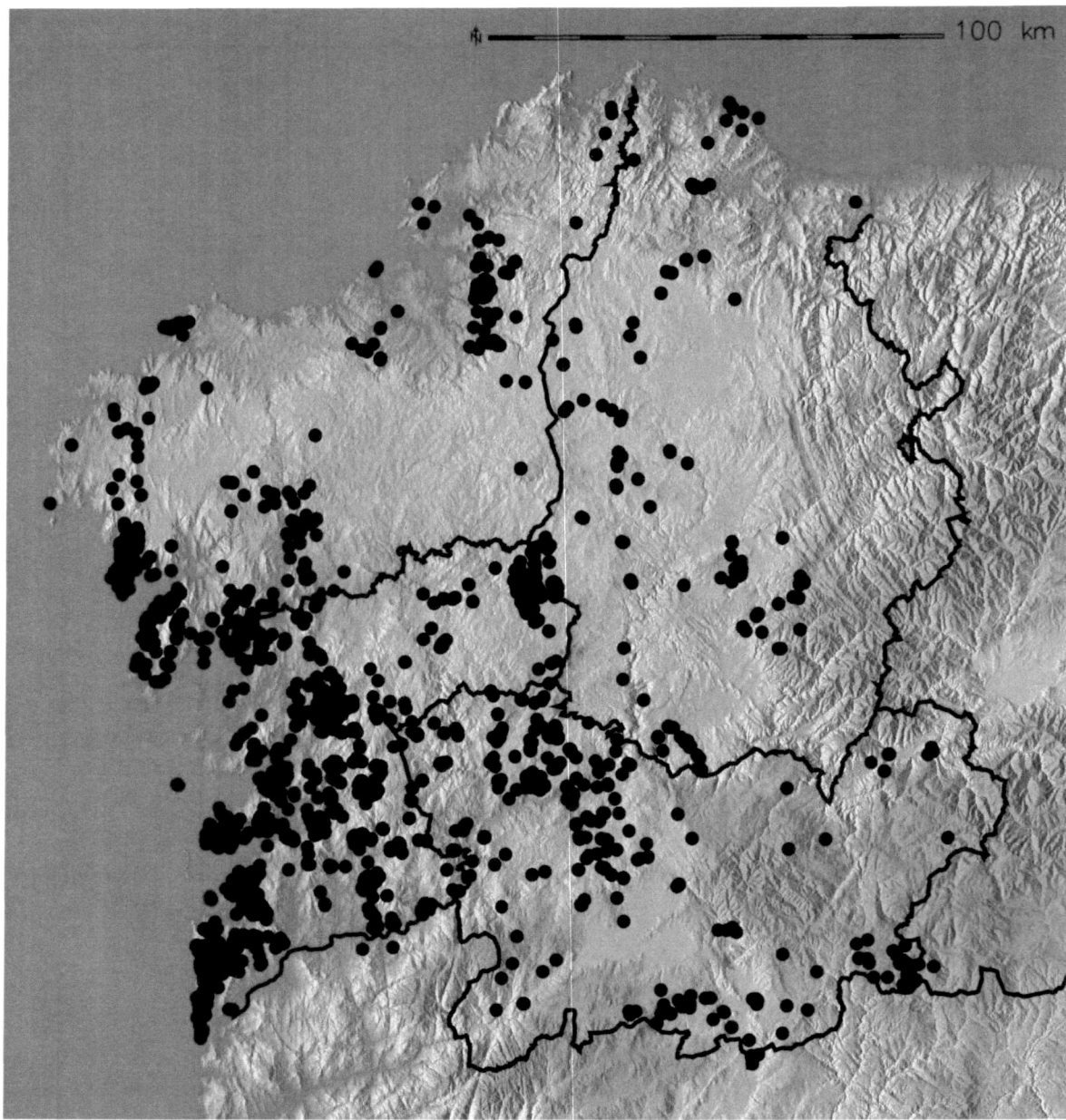

FIGURE 2. DISTRIBUTION OF THE GALICIAN PETROGLYPHS.

compared to the spatial distribution published in 1979 (Peña and Vázquez). If we consider that we counted the data in the Dirección Xeral de Patrimonio Cultural and there have not been registered all the petroglyphs in this province, this number should be increased (González Aguiar, 2011).

In quantitative terms, the distribution of petroglyphs is conditioned by the coastal proximity of the areas. This distribution is not only seen in terms of numbers, but also in the motifs that appear in the engraved panels, as we will analyse below (Peña and Rey, 2001).

Cup-marks (Table 1), the simplest motif in rock art, amounts to 61.9% of all the motifs. Its spatial distribution is not restricted to the Western area of Galicia, as it appears among the whole Galician territory.

Motifs	Number of rocks	Total percentage	Number of rocks with isolated motifs	Total percentage appearance
Cup marks	2082	61,9%	855	41,1%
Simple Circles	801	23,8%	77	9,6%
Circular Combinations	1109	33,0%	263	23,7%
Labyrinths	23	0,7%	3	13,0%
Zoomorphs	339	10,1%	96	28,3%
Halberds	24	0,7%	3	12,5%
Daggers	45	1,3%	4	8,9%
Shields	8	0,2%	1	12,5%
Crosses	668	19,9%	247	37,0%
Other prehistoric	644	19,2%	75	11,6%
Other historic	388	11,5%	112	28,9%

TABLE 1. NUMBER AND PERCENTAGE OF SITES WHERE THE DIFFERENT MOTIFS ARE PRESENT.

The second most common motifs in Galician rock art are the circular combinations (33%) and simple circles (23.8%). As they only differ in the number of circles of the composition, both motifs have been studied together in a great number of researches (Costas Goberna and Novoa Álvarez, 1993). If we take them as one motif, this would increase the percentage of appearances, which makes this motif closer in importance to cup-marks (56.8%).

Cup-marks, simple circles and circular combinations are the most spread motifs in Galicia. The relation between these motifs has been pointed out by several researchers, since it is the most representative panel of Galician rock art. However, there are some differences in the composition of these motifs in engraved panels. In coastal areas we find bigger panels with more complex combinations of the three motifs, while in inland areas the presence of these motifs is simpler.

Between geometric motifs, labyrinths (0.7%) have commanded much attention due to their peculiar design and cultural implications (Santos, 2007: 42), but its census is not as high as it is in the case of circles. Moreover, its distribution is not homogeneous, as 15 out of the 23 known rocks are in the province of Pontevedra. They seem to associate themselves preferentially with circular combinations.

If we pay attention to the chart, we find out that the motifs with less representation are the natural motifs, both zoomorphic images and weapons. The distribution of these motifs is restricted to the Western surroundings of Galicia (Rodríguez Rellán, et al. 2010). Zoomorphic images (10.1% of the representations) predominate in the Rías Baixas and more specifically in the lower part of the Lérez River, which makes it almost a coastal phenomenon, as inland regions lack of animal representations.

Even though weapons have the lower representation (2.3% out of the total), its distribution in the province of Pontevedra distances from the coast (Fábregas Valcarce, et al. 2009), while in A Coruña weapons only appear in coastal areas. Daggers (1.3%) are the most commonly represented weapons, followed by halberds (0.7%) and shield forms (0.2%). In the same rock, weapons and the called "other prehistoric" (including anthropomorphic images) usually appear together. Under the denomination "other prehistoric" are encompassed motifs such as anthropomorphic images, podomorphs and idols; that only occur individually in a few sites.

We have divided a series of motifs, of presumed historical chronology, into cruciform (19.9%) and *other historic* (11.5%); the latter, like *other prehistoric*, include assorted carvings with few effectives: board games, alphabetiforms, horseshoes, *phi* and some other images of presumably modern production. 37% of the cruciform representations are accompanied by other motifs, both of historic and prehistoric chronology. In the cases of prehistoric motifs, it has been suggested that it could be treated as a Christianisation of the rock (Peña and Vázquez, 1979: 100).

Conclusions

The statistics based on the data recorded by the Dirección Xeral de Patrimonio Cultural of the Xunta de Galicia support the province of Pontevedra as the one with more petroglyph records (Bradley and Fábregas, 1998). During the last decade, there have also been discovered petroglyphs in other provinces that had fewer records.

However, the increasing number of areas with petroglyphs does not imply that the motifs in the rocks are identical. The most repeated imagesin Galicia are geometric motifs like the circular combinations, even though this motif is less common outside the Rías Baixas, with fewer appearances in the inland areas. The commonest geometric motifs are cup-marks, whose spatial distribution is wider than circular figures. Moreover, the spatial distribution shows a preference for the coastal zones, where we noticed a quantitative difference with the interior, since the most complex panels are located on the coast and as we move inland the number of rocks plummets and the engravings become simpler.

For their part, the naturalistic motifs are present in fewer areas, as it is the case of Campo Lameiro and its surroundings. They can also be found along the coast, but become less frequent in the inland, withzones where they do not appear at all. Within this group, animals show a bigger tendency to occur along with geometric motifs (mainly circular combinations) although they also appear in isolation asignificant number of times.

Bibliography

BARANDELA RIVERO, I. & LORENZO RODRÍGUEZ, J. M. 2004. *Petroglifos de Ourense. Reflexións a un primeiro reconto da arte rupestre prehistórica na provincia*. Ourense.

BRADLEY, R. 1997. *Rock art and the prehistory of Atlantic Europe*. London/New York: Routledge.

BRADLEY, R. & FÁBREGAS VALCARCE, R. 1998. Arte rupestre e Sociedade. In *Historia da arte Galega I. Prehistoria, Arte Castrexa e Arte da Romanización* (pp. 49-64). Vigo.

CABALEIRO MANZANEDO, J.; RAMOS CALVO, A.; MIGUEL DOMÍNGUEZ, J. C. DE & VÁZQUEZ VARELA, J. M. 1976. Estudio estadístico de la asociación entre ciervos y círculos en el arte rupestre prehistórico de la provincia de Pontevedra. *Gallaecia, 2*, 117-124.

CANCELA REY, R. A.; CAROLLO LIMERES, M. C. & VÁZQUEZ VARELA, J. M. 1984. Estudio de la agrupación y asociación entre petroglifos prehistóricos de la provincia de Pontevedra. *Cuadernos de Estudios Gallegos, XXXV*, 23-30.

COSTAS GOBERNA, F. J. & NOVOA ÁLVAREZ, P. 1993. Los grabados rupestres de Galicia. *Monografías Museu Arqueolóxico e Histórico de A Coruña, 6*.

FÁBREGAS VALCARCE, R. & RODRÍGUEZ RELLÁN, C. 2012. A arte rupestre do Norte da Península do Barbanza. In R. Fábregas Valcarce & C. Rodríguez Rellán (eds.), *A arte rupestre no Norte do Barbanza*. Santiago de Compostela: Andavira.

FÁBREGAS VALCARCE, R.; RODRÍGUEZ RELLÁN, C. & RODRÍGUEZ ÁLVAREZ, E. 2009. Representacións de armas no interior de Galicia (Comarca de Deza, Pontevedra). Unha reflexión sobre a distribución e cronoloxía destes motivos. *Gallaecia, 28*, 49-68.

GARCÍA ALÉN, A. & PEÑA SANTOS, A. D. LA 1980. *Grabados rupestres de la provincia de Pontevedra*. Fundación Barrié de la Maza. Catalogación Arqueológica y Artística de Galicia del Museo de Pontevedra.

GONZÁLEZ AGUIAR, B. 2011. Grabados rupestres en el Sur de la Provincia de Lugo. *Espacio, Tiempo y Forma. Serie I. Prehistoria y Arqueología, 4*, 123-140.

GRUPO DE ARQUEOLOXÍA DA TERRA DE TRASANCOS. 2009. Novos gravados rupestres nas parroquias de Torres e Vilamateo -Concello de Vilarmaior- (I). *Anuario Brigantino, N° 32*, 11-30. Retrieved from http://www.arqueoloxia.com/publicaciones/

Grupo de Arqueoloxía Da Terra de Trasancos. 2011. Novos gravados rupestres nas parroquias de Torres e Vilamateo -Concello de Vilarmaior- (II). *Anuario Brigantino, N° 34*, 27-40. Retrieved from http://www.arqueoloxia.com/publicaciones/

Martín Sarmiento, F. 1745. *Viaje a Galicia* (1975th ed.). Museo de Pontevedra.

Martínez Salazar, A. 1898. (August 8). Prehistoria coruñesa. Las piedras con signos del Monte dos Bicos. *La Voz de Galicia, N O 5.286*. A Coruña. Retrieved from http://ahoradosmouros.blogspot.com.es/2008/12/pra-romper-un-pouco-vista.html / consultado 18 xuño 2013.

Murguía, M. 1865. *Historia de Galicia: (resumen esencial)*. Buenos Aires: Centro Gallego, 1933.

Peña Santos, A. de la & Rey García, J. M. 2001. *Petroglifos de Galicia*. Vía Láctea, A Coruña.

Peña Santos, A. de la & Vázquez Varela, J. M. 1979. *Los petroglifos gallegos. Grabados rupestres prehistóricos al aire libre en Galicia*. Sada/A Coruña: Cuadernos del Seminario de Estudios Cerámicos de Sargadelos, 30.

Rodríguez Rellán, C. & Fábregas Valcarce, R. 2013. Beyond the borders: some thoughts on Galician rock art. In M. J. Sanches (ed.), *1° Mesa-Redonda. Arte Rupestre da Pré-História e da Proto-História_ paradigmas e metodologías de registro* (pp. 239-248). Trabalhos de Arqueologia, 54.

Rodríguez Rellán, C.; Fábregas Valcarce, R.; Eiroa Pose, A.; Rodríguez Álvarez, E. & Gorgoso López, L. 2010. Alén da fronteira naturalista na arte rupestre galega. Estacións con zoomorfos na Costa da Morte (A Coruña). *Gallaecia, 29*, 83-102.

San Ildefonso Rodríguez, B. de & Tilve Jar, Á. M. 1995. Os debuxantes da "Sociedad Arqueológica" de Pontevedra. In *Os debuxantes da "Sociedad Arqueológica" de Pontevedra* (pp. 31-38). Pontevedra.

Santos Estévez, M. 2007. *Petroglifos y paisaje social en la prehistoria reciente del noroeste de la Península Ibérica. TAPA 38*. Instituto de Estudos Galegos Padre Sarmiento e CSIC. Retrieved from http://digital.csic.es/handle/10261/37908.

Sobrino Buhigas, R. 1935. *Corpus Petroglyphorum Gallaeciae*. Santiago de Compostela: Compostellae Gallaecia: Seminario de Estudos Galegos.

Vázquez Rozas, R. 1997. *Petroglifos de las Rías Baixas gallegas. Análisis artístico de un arte prehistórico*. Vigo: Diputación Provincial de Pontevedra.

Vázquez Rozas, R. 2006. Aproximación estadística a los petroglifos gallegos. *Minius XIV*, 349-364.